Praying
in the Spirit

Barry Chant

Sovereign World

Sovereign World Ltd
PO Box 777
Tonbridge
Kent TN11 0ZS
England

Unless otherwise stated, all Scripture quotations are taken from The New International Version, Copyright 1973, 1978, 1984 by the International Bible Society.

ISBN 1 85240 319 5

The publishers aim to produce books which will help to extend and build up the Kingdom of God. We do not necessarily agree with every view expressed by the author, or with every interpretation of Scripture expressed. We expect each reader to make his/her judgement in the light of their own understanding of God's Word and in an attitude of Christian love and fellowship.

Typeset by CRB Associates, Reepham, Norfolk.
Cover design by CCD, www.ccdgroup.co.uk
Printed in the United States of America

'Too often we pray to get things – healing, money, a job, more church members, solutions to problems. This is to miss the main point of prayer altogether. We pray because we must pray. We cannot live if we do not pray. We pray because through prayer we meet with God. And we pray in the Spirit because there is simply no other way to pray.'

✤ ✤ ✤

Harry: 'I know how hard you have been praying. And God is answering your prayers.'
Jack: 'That's not why I pray, Harry. I pray because I can't help myself. I pray because I'm helpless. I pray because the need flows out of me all the time, waking and sleeping. It doesn't change God; it changes me.'

(C.S. Lewis in *Shadowlands*,
Spelling Films, 1993)

✤ ✤ ✤

'You should never underestimate the power of prayer.'

(Kofi Annan, United Nations Secretary-General
prior to visiting a world trouble-spot, 1998)

✤ ✤ ✤

'Satan trembles when he sees
The weakest saint upon his knees.'

(William Cowper,
English poet and hymn-writer,
in the *Olney Hymns*, 1779)

About the Author

Barry Chant was converted to Christ as a ten-year-old at a Scripture Union camp at Victor Harbour, South Australia, in 1949. He later studied at the University of Adelaide, where he majored in history, literature and education, graduating with a Bachelor of Arts with honours and a Diploma in Education. He then studied for a Bachelor of Divinity degree through the Melbourne College of Divinity while working as a secondary school teacher. He later completed a Doctor of Ministry degree from Luther Rice Seminary, Florida, USA, and a Doctor of Philosophy degree from Macquarie University, New South Wales (2000).

From 1963, he pioneered and pastored several churches until 1979, when he founded Tabor College, a multidenominational Christian education ministry with campuses in four Australian cities – Adelaide, Melbourne, Perth and Sydney. He is a regular speaker at seminars, conferences and church services in many denominations.

Barry Chant has written over a dozen books ranging from theology to church history to victorious living to family life, including the popular *Spindles* series for children. He is married to Vanessa and they have three adult children and a growing number of grandchildren.

Contents

Chapter 1

'When You Pray, Say: "Father..."'
(Luke 11:2)

Why pray? The greater question is, why not?

At the turn of the millennium, there was an exciting refocusing on prayer. All over the world, people were praying more than ever before. Many Christian organizations and associations were marshalling people to redouble their efforts to pray for the world.

In 1994, 115,000 prayer guides were distributed worldwide in ten languages for people to pray for Muslim countries.[1] On 25 June of that year, an estimated twelve million Christians in 179 countries took to the streets to march in witness for Jesus and to pray together for their cities and countries. Many concluded with all-night prayer vigils.

In the same year, some 1,200 people from thirty-two nations were involved in prayer teams that visited sixty-two of the least evangelized countries of the world. At the same time, millions of people were involved in 'praying through the Window' – that is, praying for the inhabitants of the so-called '10/40 Window', that part of the world which has been least touched by the gospel. In Korea, in late 1994, one million people attended a single prayer meeting.

One of the best-selling books of the 1990s was Patrick Johnstone's *Operation World*,[2] a manual for prayer for world evangelization. Journals and periodicals were published which instructed believers in how to pray intelligently for the peoples of the world.

According to *Christianity Today* 'millions of Christian believers' were holding 'mass prayer rallies world-wide' and 'scholars
and prayer-movement leaders [were] asking whether this
development foreshadows church renewal on a global scale'.[3]
The article goes on to quote David Barrett as claiming that 160
million Christians worldwide were committed to daily prayer
for revival and that there are some 1,300 global prayer networks
and ten million prayer groups which 'have revival on their
agenda'.

International groups co-ordinated major conferences and
prayer gatherings such as the Global Consultation on World
Evangelization in Pretoria, South Africa, in 1997 and the
Amsterdam 2000 conference for preaching evangelists hosted
by the Billy Graham Evangelistic Association and attended by
thousands. Undeniable visitations occurred in Argentina, Indo-
nesia and China. Bible Colleges throughout Australia reported
record enrolments. Evangelists such as Reinhard Bonnke were
leading millions to Christ.[4] Thousands of people were involved
in aspects of what came to be called the 'Toronto Blessing' and
the 'Pensacola Revival', which in spite of extremist elements
nevertheless touched many with a renewed passion to wait on
God.

In the year 2001, the Australian Pentecostal Ministers' Fellowship organized Ozpray, a chain of prayer where, every day of the
year, several churches prayed through the whole twenty-four
hours. The result was an unbroken chain of prayer for 365 days
involving hundreds of churches and thousands of people. This
initiative was continued on into the twenty-first century.

Ever since the Pentecostal revival at the turn of the twentieth
century, more and more believers have experienced a fresh
infilling of the Holy Spirit. It is now almost commonplace to
talk about the Spirit-filled life. Terms like 'baptized in the Holy
Spirit' and 'filled with the Spirit' are regularly heard in both
pulpit and pew. And so is the expression 'pray in the Spirit'.

What does it mean to pray in the Spirit? Is it just a synonym
for speaking in tongues? For fervour and enthusiasm? For
passion and zeal? For divinely inspired praying? For intercession? Is spiritual praying different from other kinds of prayer?
How do we do it? What are the benefits? What are the results?
How and when should we do it? How do we hear from God?

What about visions and dreams? How do we pray for others? Why do we need to pray for others? How can prayer become more spiritual? More fulfilling? These and many other questions like them are addressed in this book.

Right at the beginning it is important to state clearly that praying in the Spirit is not an option. It is essential for every Christian to pray in the Spirit. Scripture commands it (Ephesians 6:18) and life demands it. It is not something we can leave to spiritual 'experts'. It is not just for 'intercessors'. It is not just for apostles or prophets or pastors. Prayer in the Spirit is for everyone.

There are many excellent reasons why we need to pray in the Spirit whenever we can. But before we ask why we should pray in the Spirit, we need to ask a more fundamental question, namely, why should we pray at all? If God knows everything anyway, what is the point of prayer? Why should we have to ask Him to do what a loving God would want to do in any case? If God already knows our needs, what is the point of telling Him?

The best way to answer this question is to ask another one: Why should children talk to their parents? Don't loving parents already know their needs? Aren't they already willing to help them and provide for them in every way?

Prayer is more than vocalizing needs. It is not just asking. In essence prayer is fellowship – fellowship between a loving Father and His children. When we pray, we draw near to God. Like small children, we sneak up to our Father and cling to Him, deriving strength, reassurance and warmth just from being with Him. As Hallesby puts it, 'God has designed prayer as a means of intimate and joyous fellowship between God and man.' [5] And Rinker writes, 'Prayer is the expression of the human heart in conversation with God ... prayer is a dialogue between two persons who love each other.' [6]

From this perspective, the question 'Why pray?' becomes almost redundant. Why do children talk to their parents? Why do sweethearts spend hours just being together? Why do friends look forward to shared social events? Why do marriage partners ache with loneliness whenever they are separated? Why do God's people love to spend time with Him?

Prayer is essentially communion with God. We love to pray because we love God. And if we love God we love to be in His

presence. If there were no other reason for praying, that would
be enough.

Prayer gives us perspective

Prayer gives us perspective. Through prayer, we see ourselves as
we really are before God. When we forget God, it is easy for us to
have a distorted and inflated idea of our own importance.
When we choose to spend time with Him, however, we are
brought face to face with the reality of our own insignificance.
As we ponder His greatness we realize how feeble and helpless
we are. For the psalmist, even the contemplation of creation
was enough to overawe him:

> 'O LORD, our Lord,
>   how majestic is your name in all the earth!
> You have set your glory above the heavens...
> When I consider your heavens,
>   the work of your fingers,
> the moon and the stars,
>   which you have set in place,
> what is man that you are mindful of him,
>   the son of man that you care for him?'   (Psalm 8:1, 3–4)

How much more does an audience with God Himself overwhelm
us with a shattering recognition of His glory and majesty!

Furthermore, as we are confronted with God's holiness, we
see our desperate need of Him. Like John, we fall at His feet as
though dead in terror of the pristine purity of His countenance
and the blazing glory of His holiness (Revelation 1:12–17).
David Yonggi Cho, whose astonishing church and ministry in
Korea has been largely built on prayer, writes: 'When you come
in contact with God in your time of prayer, the first thing you
feel in your heart, as you enter into His divine presence, is a
realization of your sin. No one can sense pride in the presence
of a holy God.'[7] Prayer is vital for it reminds us constantly of
the true nature of things and where we stand in the order of the
universe.

This was Job's experience. When he was confronted with the
greatness of God, he humbled himself in awe at the greatness of

His majesty (Job 38:1ff.). I remember reading this passage some years ago and feeling something of my own insignificance in the light of God's infinite person and power. As I prayed, I had a sense of being overawed and overwhelmed by the immeasurable, omnipotent presence of the Lord. I was not intimidated – the experience was strangely pleasing – but I was reminded of my own need to tread gently before the great God and Creator of the universe. I saw how perilous it would be to attempt even the slightest departure from His will.

Through prayer we obtain forgiveness

Knowing the holiness of God convinces us of our desperate need of forgiveness. Like the tax collector in the parable of Jesus, we dare not even look up to heaven, but beat our breasts and cry, *'God, have mercy on me, a sinner'* (Luke 18:13). A missionary friend of mine put it plainly when he said, 'When I come into the presence of God, I am undone!'

Then when we hear the great, good news that Christ died for our sins and that through Christ all sins are forgiven, it is through prayer that we appropriate and receive forgiveness from God (Matthew 6:12; Luke 11:4).

We rejoice that our sins are forgiven. On the cross, Christ died for the sins of every human being (Romans 5:1ff.). Through Him, all humankind is reconciled to God (2 Corinthians 5:19). But it is still necessary to come to God in repentance and faith for that forgiveness to become a reality (Acts 2:38). So we hear the encouraging words of the gospel,

'If we confess our sins, he is faithful and just and will forgive us our sins and purify us from all unrighteousness.' (1 John 1:9)

When we pray, we are able to repent and confess. Praying makes forgiveness a practical reality for us. The writer to the Hebrews puts it clearly,

'Let us draw near to God with a sincere heart in full assurance of faith, having our hearts sprinkled to cleanse us from a guilty conscience and having our bodies washed with pure water.'
(Hebrews 10:22)

Forgiveness is not a reward for our praying. It is the free, gracious gift of God. But if we do not pray, we cannot receive it. We are like children who have gone our own way. Prayer is the means by which we make contact with our loving Father who wants to welcome us home once again.

Such praying can be very simple, of course. I once heard an ex-alcoholic testify of his deliverance. He had reached terrible depths of addiction – even to the extent of spreading boot polish on bread to satisfy his craving. One evening he wandered into a church. He saw the joy on people's faces and the well-being of their demeanour. So he prayed, 'Righto, Sport, you did it for them, do it for me.' And God did! He has been free from alcohol ever since. It was hardly a proper prayer. But God heard the spirit behind it and responded in a loving and powerful way.

Through prayer we gain access to God

Prayer enables us to gain access to the Father. When parents and children do not communicate there are usually problems. In fact, when a father and a son are 'not talking', it is a serious matter. It seems both unnatural and unacceptable.

As members of God's family, we need to keep in close touch with Him – to be in communion with Him all the time. Prayer is essential for this. *'Come near to God and he will come near to you,'* writes James (James 4:8). If we want intimacy with the Father, we must pray. We must spend time with Him. We must linger longer in His presence.

Sometimes, Jesus prayed all night, so precious was His time with God (Luke 6:12). Virtually one whole chapter of the Bible is devoted to the great prayer that Jesus offered to His Father (John 17). It is important to note how often Jesus calls God 'Father' in this prayer (vv. 1, 5, 11, 24, 25). There is no question about His relationship with God. It was a family affair. Jesus plainly saw Himself as a Son who had rights of access to His Father at any time. This same access is given to us. Through Christ, we have gained access by faith into the grace in which we stand (Romans 5:2).

When my wife and I used to run a small delicatessen, customers were not permitted behind the counter. This especially applied to the local children who would have loved to get in among the stocks of sweets and drinks and chips. When we were serving our customers, we had to keep our eye on their children, in case they crept behind us when we weren't looking! But our own children were always allowed in. They had access. It was not that they were any better behaved or more deserving than the other children. It was just that they had a relationship with us which put them in a different category.

When they came home from school, we didn't interrogate them to see if they had behaved themselves properly during the day. We didn't demand acceptable levels of performance with their schoolwork before we would admit them. They just walked straight in! Past the customers, past the shop counter and into the house. Usually, even if we were busy, we would stop and hug them. Because they were our children, they had access to us in a way that no other children in the neighbourhood had.

In the same way, we have access to the Father. Not on the basis of any deserving or merit on our part, but simply because we are His children. But we should never take this privilege for granted. It is through prayer that this access becomes a reality. If the divine Son of God needed to spend prime time with His Father, how much more do we?

Through prayer we express our dependency on God

Prayer expresses our dependency on God. Talking with the Father enables us to articulate our need of Him in our lives.

This is more important for us than for God. He is only too well aware of our helpless state. But we sometimes forget it! Jesus reminds us very plainly that apart from Him we can do nothing (John 15:5). In our thinking, we tend to qualify this by assuming that He didn't really mean **absolutely** nothing, but that we can still do **some** things on our own. The Lord's words stand, however. As far as God is concerned, all our achievements apart from Christ are valueless. They might as well not happen. From an eternal perspective, without Him, we really can do nothing.

We are like a teenage girl who has run away from home. She might do well at her studies, gain exceptional employment and earn a high salary. She might even be an influence for good in the community. But as long as she is away from home and out of fellowship with her family, to them all the rest is worthless. Until she is reconciled, nothing else matters. But when reconciliation takes place, everything takes on a new value, and her previous 'good works' now do become genuinely good. It is the relationship that makes the difference.

When we pray, we realize how much we need God and how much we need to be in fellowship with Him. In difficult times, we don't know what to do or how to cope, but like Jehoshaphat, our eyes are on the Lord (2 Chronicles 20:5ff.).

> *'Let us then approach the throne of grace with confidence, so that we may receive mercy and find grace to help us in our time of need.'*   (Hebrews 4:16)

Through prayer we receive guidance

We can only know the will of God when we really know God. This is a truism, but even so it needs to be stated. To use the analogy of human relationships once again, when we really know someone, we also know what they want. We can anticipate their needs or preferences. We know without being told what they are thinking and how they are feeling.

This is what happens in marriage. After years of living together, you don't have to ask your partner what she would like to do or where she would like to go or what she would like to eat. You know all this because you know her.

So the more time we spend in prayer, the more we learn the will of God. What the Father desires becomes what we desire. The Father's purposes become our purposes. What moves the heart of God moves our hearts.

This is beautifully expressed in Psalm 84. Here one of the sons of Korah tells how he loves to spend time with God. He sees a little bird that has made its nest by the altar of God and longs for a similar closeness with the Lord. He knows that those who dwell in God's house are guided through life. They are specially blessed. This point is emphasized by the use of the musical term *'selah'* which possibly indicates the need to pause and reflect. Those who find their strength in God turn valleys of tears into fountains of joy. They go from strength to strength and eventually reach their heavenly home:

> 'How lovely is your dwelling place,
>   O LORD Almighty!
> My soul yearns, even faints,
>   for the courts of the LORD;
> my heart and my flesh cry out
>   for the living God.
> Even the sparrow has found a home,
>   and the swallow a nest for herself,
>   where she may have her young –
> a place near your altar,
>   O LORD Almighty, my King and my God.
> Blessed are those who dwell in your house;
>   they are ever praising you.   Selah.
> Blessed are those whose strength is in you,
>   who have set their hearts on pilgrimage.
> As they pass through the Valley of Baca,
>   they make it a place of springs;
>   the autumn rains also cover it with pools.
> They go from strength to strength,
>   till each appears before God in Zion.'   (Psalm 84:1–7)

So, too, as we spend time in prayer, we are guided by God (Romans 8:14). Prayer greatly increases the possibility of the Lord's voice reaching us. It was when Peter was praying that the Lord spoke to him (Acts 10:10ff.). Similarly, it was when a group of prophets and teachers at Antioch were worshipping the Lord that the Holy Spirit gave them direction (Acts 13:1ff.). Prayer enhances our ability to hear from God.

Through prayer we express our fellowship with one another

We have already seen how prayer is crucial for our fellowship with the Father. It is also vital for our fellowship with one another.

We may be separated from others through distance or circumstances. Or, we may want to help a brother or a sister, but do

not know how. Even if we can do nothing else, we can pray for
them. Through prayer we express our concern for others. This is
especially true for leaders. We need to uphold them, that they
might faithfully discharge their duties. In many cases, in the
very nature of things, this is all we can do. Often, because of
their work, it is impossible to spend time together with them.
But through prayer, we can still develop a mutual fellowship.

On many occasions, Paul urges us to do this. He pleads with
the Ephesians and the Colossians and the Thessalonians to pray
for him and his fellow-workers (Ephesians 6:18, 19; Colossians
4:2–4, 12ff.; 1 Thessalonians 5:25; 2 Thessalonians 3:1). He asks
them to pray:

- for Paul himself (Ephesians 6:19; Colossians 4:3)
- for his team (1 Thessalonians 5:25)
- for words to be given him (Ephesians 6:19)
- for a door to open for the message (Colossians 4:3)
- for him to speak fearlessly (Ephesians 6:19, 20)
- for him to make known the mystery of the gospel
  (Ephesians 6:20)
- for him to proclaim the mystery of Christ (Colossians 4:3)
- for him to proclaim Christ clearly (Colossians 4:4)
- that the message of the Lord may spread rapidly
  (2 Thessalonians 3:1)
- that the message of the Lord may be honoured
  (2 Thessalonians 3:1).

He also urges us to pray for all those in authority (1 Timothy
2:1ff.). James tells us to pray for one another (James 5:14ff.).

One of the most challenging statements about prayer ever
made is found in the words of the prophet Samuel,

> *'As for me, far be it from me that I should sin against the* LORD
> *by failing to pray for you.'*   (1 Samuel 12:23)

Not only do we need to express our fellowship for one another
in prayer, but not to do so is a sin against God.

Through prayer we identify with the needs of others

There are several striking cases in Scripture of people praying for others so strongly they identified with their needs.

Moses often pleaded with God on behalf of his people. Time and again he prayed for them and asked God to bless them or rescue them or forgive them. The most graphic example occurred when Moses returned from Sinai with the two tablets of stone containing the Ten Commandments. To his intense dismay and great disappointment, during his absence the people had turned away from God and made themselves idols of gold (Exodus 32).

It is hard to imagine what Moses must have felt. He had just spent six long weeks in one of the most awe-inspiring, barren, harsh, arid places in the world. He had suffered the extremes of desert temperatures. He had gone without food or drink (Exodus 24:18; 34:28; Deuteronomy 9:9, 18). He had sacrificed personal comfort and basic human needs so he could hear from God and correctly lead his people. And when he returned, what did he find? Celebration, dancing, immoral practices and feasting. While he was suffering privation for them, they were having a party!

Everything within him must have felt like turning his back on these ungracious and disloyal people. Certainly he was angry – angry enough to mete out punishment on thousands of them. But, astonishingly, after this he said to them,

> 'You have committed a great sin. But now I will go up to the LORD; perhaps I can make atonement for your sin.'   (Exodus 32:30)

What an extraordinary response. It would be hard to blame Moses if he asked God to release him from the responsibility of leading the Israelites and for them to be disenfranchised as the chosen people. But he does the very opposite. He asks God to forgive them!

This is a remarkable example of grace and tolerance. But Moses goes even further. When he does pray, he not only asks for the sins of the Israelites to be dismissed, but goes on to offer himself as an atoning sacrifice in their place!

> *'So Moses went back to the* Lord *and said, "Oh, what a great sin these people have committed! They have made themselves gods of gold. But now, please forgive their sin – but if not, then blot me out of the book you have written."'*   (Exodus 32:31–32)

God did not allow Moses to do this. But his willingness is the striking thing. He so truly identified with these people that he was willing to give his own life if it would save theirs.

It takes extraordinary love and compassion to pray like this. This is why it is important to pray in the Spirit. Without the Spirit's help, it is virtually impossible.

Daniel was another who knew how to identify with his people. Together with thousands of his compatriots, he was an exile in Babylon. The many sins of Judah had resulted in the destruction of Jerusalem and the decimation of the nation (2 Kings 24:3–4).

It would have been easy for Daniel to blame everyone else for his plight. After all, he was one of the few upright people in the nation. When others rebelled against God, or sacrificed to idols, or shed innocent blood, or committed sins of the flesh, he remained faithful, true and godly. He could easily have prayed:

> '**They** have sinned and done wrong. **They** have been wicked and have rebelled; **they** have turned away from your commands and laws. **They** have not listened to your servants the prophets ... Lord, you are righteous, but this day **they** are covered with shame ... **they** and **their** kings, **their** princes and **their** fathers are covered with shame because **they** have sinned against you ... **they** have rebelled ... **they** have not obeyed the Lord **their** God or kept the laws he gave **them** through his servants the prophets.'

It is remarkable to see what he did pray:

> *'**We** have sinned and done wrong. **We** have been wicked and have rebelled; **we** have turned away from your commands and laws. **We** have not listened to your servants the prophets ... Lord, you are righteous, but this day **we** are covered with shame ... **we** and **our** kings, **our** princes and **our** fathers are covered with shame because **we** have sinned against you ... **we** have*

*rebelled; **we** have not obeyed the LORD **our** God or kept the laws
he gave **us** through his servants the prophets.'*   (Daniel 9:5ff.)

Daniel clearly and plainly identified himself with his people.
Their sins were his sins; their failures were his failures. He did
not point the finger at them and condemn them, much as he
had the right to do so. Rather, he shared the blame. He saw
himself as one with them and repented on their behalf.

Through prayer we are able to identify with the needs of our
brothers and sisters. Rather than praying **for** them, we pray
with them. We weep at the altar together. We humble ourselves
before God together. We plead for God's mercy together.

In Daniel's case, after continuing to lament the sins of his
people, he then cried out to God on their behalf:

*'We do not make requests of you because we are righteous, but
because of your great mercy. O Lord, listen! O Lord, forgive!
O Lord, hear and act! For your sake, O my God, do not delay,
because your city and your people bear your Name.'*

(Daniel 9:18–19)

Not on the basis of his integrity. Certainly not on that of the
people. But purely on the basis of God's mercy, he pleads for
acceptance.

All prayer finds itself ultimately at the same place. It is never
by works of righteousness that we have done, but always and
only on the basis of God's great love and mercy towards us.

Paul was another who was willing to lose all for the sake of
the people he loved. *'I could wish that I myself were cursed,'* he
wrote, *'and cut off from Christ for the sake of my brothers, those of
my own race, the people of Israel'* (Romans 9:3–4a).

But it was Jesus who most fully identified with us. Not only
by His living, but by His dying. Not only by His teaching, but by
His suffering. Not only by His praying, but by His sacrificial
atoning. In becoming a human being, Christ identified totally
with us. He was willing to lose everything for the sake of
winning us back to God. The biblical term *kenosis* ('emptying')
conveys this concept very well. In order to become one with us,
Jesus 'emptied Himself' and took on Himself human form, in
order to redeem us back to God:

'*Who, being in very nature God,*
   did not consider equality with God something to be grasped,
but made himself nothing,
   taking the very nature of a servant,
   being made in human likeness.
And being found in appearance as a man,
   he humbled himself
   and became obedient to death – even death on a cross!'
                                          (Philippians 2:6–8)

There are five phases here in Christ's *kenosis*. First, He *'made himself nothing'* (literally 'emptied Himself'). Then He enslaved Himself (literally 'took the nature of a slave'). Third, He identified Himself (took human likeness). Fourth, He humbled Himself. Last, He gave Himself.

There is a pattern here, as much as it is possible for us to follow. When we identify with others like this through our prayers, we are praying very much in the spirit of Jesus.

Don't forget

- Through prayer we experience communion with God.
- Prayer gives us perspective.
- Through prayer we obtain forgiveness.
- Through prayer we gain access to God.
- Through prayer we express our dependency upon God.
- Through prayer we obtain guidance.
- Through prayer we express our fellowship with one another.
- Through prayer we identify with the needs of others.

Notes

1   South Pacific Prayer Network, *Prayerlink*, Mount Gravatt, Qld, 1:4.
2   OM Publishing, 1993.
3   14 November 1994.

4   Reinhard Bonnke's organization, Christ for All Nations, reported that over five million people completed inquiry cards during the first half of the decade.

5   O. Hallesby, *Prayer* (IVF, 1948), p. 10.

6   R. Rinker, *Prayer: Conversing with God* (Grand Rapids: Zondervan, 1959), p. 23.

7   P.Y. Cho, *Praying With Jesus* (Word, 1987), p. 24.

Chapter 2

'My Soul Thirsts for God...'
(Psalm 42:2)

Without prayer we perish

All living creatures need sustenance. If we don't eat or drink, we die. In the same way, we need spiritual nourishment. Without it, we perish. This is another reason why we should pray.

Prayer is a source of spiritual nourishment

Our major source of spiritual nourishment is the Word of God. *'Man does not live on bread alone,'* said Jesus, *'but on every word that comes from the mouth of God'* (Matthew 4:4). The prophet Jeremiah told how God's words were like delightful food to him (Jeremiah 15:16).

So we are also nourished through prayer. When we pray, we not only talk to God but we hear from Him, too. As we commune with Him, our souls are fed and our spirits refreshed. This has nowhere been better expressed than in the words of the psalmist:

> *'As the deer pants for streams of water,*
> *so my soul pants for you, O God.*
> *My soul thirsts for God, for the living God.*
> *When can I go and meet with God?'*   (Psalm 42:1–2)

The hunger of David's soul for God is like an exhausted animal's thirst for flowing, life-giving water. In another psalm David takes this even further. When he was in the wilderness of Judah, a dry, rocky, barren place where the heat is intense and there are few springs, his longing for God was even greater than his thirst for water:

> 'O God, you are my God,
>   earnestly I seek you;
> my soul thirsts for you,
>   my body longs for you,
> in a dry and weary land
>   where there is no water.'   (Psalm 63:1)

David realized that even if his body was saved, he could not survive without God. He had seen the power and glory of God and he knew that he could not live without it. For the loving kindness of God is better than life itself (Psalm 63:3) and, through God, his soul would be satisfied *'as with the richest of foods'* (Psalm 63:5). There are so many substitutes for spiritual sustenance these days. Billheimer asks:

> 'If we didn't have such a high standard of living would we not have more time to pray? If we were not so intoxicated with travel, pleasure, vacations and recreation, would we not have more time to pray? We are not only cheating God and the world but we are cheating ourselves. By our failure to pray we are frustrating God's high purpose in the ages. We are robbing the world of God's best plan for it and we are limiting our rank in eternity.' [1]

Such hunger and thirst for God is the essence of true prayer. Jesus said,

> 'Blessed are those who hunger and thirst for righteousness,
>   for they will be filled.'   (Matthew 5:6)

We need to pray to draw on God for spiritual nourishment and the sustenance of our spiritual lives. The truth is, our prayer habits reflect the degree of our hunger for God. The more we pray, the more we display our passion for Him. Prayer, then, becomes a barometer of our spirituality.

There is a strange irony here. The more we pray, the more our sense of need to pray increases. The more we satisfy our hunger, the hungrier we become. And the reverse is also true. The less we pray, the less we feel the need to do so. We would think it would be otherwise. But it is not. This is why sinners can go for years without a conscious prayer and not feel the lack of it, whereas saints will lament even a few moments of absence from God.

Prayer is the cry of the heart which yearns for the satisfaction that is only found in God. As Augustine put it centuries ago, 'You have created us for yourself and our hearts are restless till we find our rest in you.'[2]

One danger we face is praying only for a particular purpose. True prayer is a matter of spiritual health. And we need to be healthy to live an effective Christian life. It is like breathing. We don't breathe just so we can walk or talk or play sport or make love or watch a film or read a book. We breathe so we can live. If we live, then we can do those other things. Neither do we pray just so we can preach a sermon or lead a youth group or face a difficult task or be relieved from pain or find a life's partner. We pray so we can live an effective spiritual life. When this is accomplished the other things all find their place. They become benefits of our prayer, not the reason for it.

When I am teaching homiletics, I warn my students against the dangers of waiting until just before they preach to pray. They need to have a sustained prayer life so that whenever they are called on to preach, spiritually at least, they are ready.

Prayer needs to be woven into the fabric of our lives so that wherever we are and whatever we are doing, it is a spontaneous and instinctive part of our behaviour. Between times, when we are walking down a corridor or standing under the shower or waiting for a traffic light to change or listening to a recorded message on the telephone, our natural inclination should be to pray. Our hearts should spontaneously begin to worship the Lord and our lips to utter His praise. We should not need to make a conscious decision to do it. Prayer should be such a part of us that, like breathing, it should just happen automatically, sustaining us all the time.

Through prayer we draw spiritual strength

We draw spiritual strength through prayer. On the one hand, we gain an appreciation of our own inabilities when we pray; on the other we tap into the enormous resources of God. The most graphic biblical example of this can be found in the life of Jesus. In those terrible hours in Gethsemane, just prior to the crucifixion, Jesus offered anguished prayers to the Father for the strength to proceed unflinchingly to the cross. Through praying, He was fortified and sustained (Matthew 26:36ff.). When His disciples fell asleep, He encouraged them to find strength in the same way,

> *'Watch and pray, so that you will not fall into temptation. The spirit is willing, but the body is weak.'*   (Matthew 26:41)

Both the verbs Jesus uses here are present imperatives which imply a sense of continuity. In other words, the actions of watching and praying are not to be isolated, individual events but ongoing, regular practice. Interestingly, the English name 'Gregory' is derived from the Greek word for 'watch' which means to 'be awake', to 'be watchful or attentive', to 'be vigilant or circumspect'. As we give ourselves to thoughtful, attentive prayer, we will be protected from temptation and strengthened spiritually. It is no wonder we fall into sin if our prayer lives are emaciated. In our human frailty, prayer is one means by which we are built up.

It is interesting that Paul specifically names prayer in tongues as a means of strengthening (1 Corinthians 14:4a). If we are spiritually weak, we need to pray.

Through prayer we claim the blessings of God

The teaching of the New Testament is very plain that we are richly blessed in Christ. Indeed, through Him, every possible blessing is already ours (Ephesians 1:3). In Christ we are chosen, predestined, adopted, redeemed, forgiven, graced, enlightened, included in Christ, sealed by the Holy Spirit, raised and seated in heavenly places. We have a calling filled with hope, a glorious inheritance and infinite resources to accomplish the work of God. We share the authority of Christ over every evil work. We have been brought into fellowship with people of every race and colour. We have been built into a holy temple to the Lord (Ephesians 1:1–2:22). There is nothing more God can do for us. Many people, however, are living in ignorance of these blessings. Others know about them but have never claimed them. Through prayer, we are able to draw near to God and lay hold of the blessings that are already ours in Christ.

Of course, this also requires faith to believe the Word of God. We need the Holy Spirit, as we shall see, to enable us to appropriate the goodness of God on our behalf. But the starting point is prayer. If we don't pray, we cannot fully exercise our faith.

As we pray, we tap into God's blessings. They are all ours already through Christ but in this way we make them ours in reality. So, in his letter to the Ephesians, Paul tells them how he never stops praying for them to receive the blessings of God in their lives and urges them, too, to pray (Ephesians 1:17ff.; 3:14ff.; 6:18). He asks God that *'the eyes of their hearts'* may be enlightened as they receive a spirit of wisdom and revelation in the knowledge of Christ (Ephesians 1:15ff.).

We need to pray the same prayer for ourselves. It is the Spirit who opens our eyes and reveals the things of God to us (1 Corinthians 2:9–11). But it is by prayer that we position ourselves so the Spirit can do so. If we don't pray, we necessarily and needlessly close ourselves off from much of what the Holy Spirit wants to show us and do in us (Ephesians 3:14–21).

This is why many people are living below the victory level. All the resources we need are promised to us in Christ, but if we do not appropriate them in prayer, by faith, they might as well not exist for us at all. Too often we are like people with a fortune in the bank who never visit the agency to make a withdrawal. Or like a starving family who do not know that their pantry is bulging with food.

Every blessing is supplied for us in Christ. We claim those blessings by faith. And faith is expressed through prayer. An old gospel song puts it like this:

'Prayer is the key to heaven
But faith unlocks the door.'

Without faith, we cannot please God (Hebrews 11:6); but without prayer, we cannot exercise faith. So Jesus said,

> 'Therefore I tell you, whatever you ask for in prayer, believe that you have received it, and it will be yours.' (Mark 11:24)

We need to do what Jesus said.

Prayer is an act of obedience

We pray because we are told to do so! Prayer is an act of obedience. If there were no other reason for praying, this would be enough. Too often we want reasons for things. No doubt this is part of our modern living. We no longer accept traditional practices just because we have always done them that way. Nowadays, we want to know why. Sometimes, it is as though we are trying to reinvent the wheel. But it is for our benefit that God instructs us to pray. There is comfort in knowing what is right.

Part of the dilemma of the post-modern society is that there has been an erosion of standards and sometimes we no longer know what is true and what is false. Whatever pleases us is deemed to be right. One person's 'truth' is as good as another's. Absolutes have often been abandoned and relativity rules unchallenged. It is an act of God's kindness to command us to pray. Bingham writes:

> 'That God commands us is His good grace for us. We would not feel secure if we were not commanded. If we had to operate only upon our own understandings, whims and inclinations then we would have little peace.' [3]

Not that it is a sin to challenge the reason for doing something. There is nothing wrong with asking questions. I regularly urge my students to do so. If what we are teaching them is false, it needs to be questioned. How else can error be detected and refuted? On the other hand, if what we are teaching is true, it can face any question. Truth has nothing to fear from questions. In this way, truth can be recognized and trusted. So either way we gain.

Sometimes there is no other explanation for why we do certain things than that it is right to do so. When a child asks,

'Why?', his mother might answer, 'Just because.' On occasions, God says something like that. What He tells us, in effect, is, 'Do it because I say so.'

When I was a boy, I attended a Boys Club at our Baptist church where the motto was, 'Do right because it is right.' At the time, I didn't understand it. It was only in later years that I realized its significance. If something is right, then we need to do it, regardless. No other justification or rationalization is necessary. When we are tempted to ask that all too popular question of post-modern life, 'What's in it for me?' the answer is, 'What difference does it make? Do it anyway!'

Prayer is like that. We have already noted many benefits of praying. But even if there were none, we would still pray, just because God tells us to do so.

So Jesus enjoined us to pray always and never give up (Luke 18:1). Paul urges us to *'pray continually'* (1 Thessalonians 5:17) and to pray on all occasions for all the saints (Ephesians 6:18) and for all those in authority (1 Timothy 2:1ff.).

Prayer is not an option. It is a divine obligation. We pray because it is the right thing to do.

Prayer pleases God

Prayer pleases God. It is as simple as that. Pray, says Paul, for *'this is good and pleases God our Saviour'* (1 Timothy 2:3).

Of course, whenever we are obedient, we honour the Lord. But prayer is particularly pleasing to Him for it is not only an act of obedience, it is also an act of intimacy. It brings us together. And there is no doubt that our heavenly Father enjoys this.

The whole redemption story is one of God's initiative in bridging the gap between heaven and earth. Because sin separates us from God, and because human beings are incapable of bridging the gap, God Himself intervened in a most extraordinary fashion. He identified with us. He became one of us. He took our place. He Himself acted as our representative. But the problem is that God cannot truly represent human beings. So He sent His only Son to be born, to live and to die among us. In this way, He was able to act on our behalf.

As a man, He was qualified to represent us. As God, He was able to represent us. As a man, He most truly shared our humanity. As God, He most powerfully expressed His deity. As true Man, He had the right to bear our guilt; as true God He had the capacity to do so. And in this mystery of godliness, He both became flesh and died for our sins and then rose again to overcome them forever. So the scripture says:

> *'Since we have now been justified by his blood, how much more shall we be saved from God's wrath through him! For if, when we were God's enemies, we were reconciled to him through the death of his Son, how much more, having been reconciled, shall we be saved through his life! Not only is this so, but we also rejoice in God through our Lord Jesus Christ, through whom we have now received reconciliation.'*   (Romans 5:9–11)

When we pray, we respond to this great act of reconciliation. It is very little compared with what God has done. But it is all we can do. And God is pleased when we do it.

Prayer gives us a sense of dignity

Knowing that God wants us to pray gives us a sense of worth and dignity. This is true of any encounter with any great person. We are not at all surprised when friends at our own level come to visit us. But if some famous person contacts us, we are both astonished and honoured.

Some years ago, my son called me to the phone. 'It's somebody named Orr,' he said. 'Oh, it's probably Dr J. Edwin Orr, the historian,' I replied jokingly, and picked up the phone to see who it really was. To my utter astonishment, it was Dr Orr! He was passing through the airport in our city and phoned to tell me that in his latest publication on revival he had quoted from a book I had written. As a young, unknown author, I was surprised and greatly honoured that he should have done this.

To be able to talk one-to-one with the Lord of heaven is a far, far greater honour! What an incredible privilege! If God wants to commune with us, then how He must value us. Again, we are reminded of David's question,

> *'what is man that you are mindful of him,
> the son of man that you care for him?'*   (Psalm 8:4)

No wonder David goes on to say,

> '*You made him a little lower than the heavenly beings
>   and crowned him with glory and honour.*'   (Psalm 8:5)

This is truly how we feel when we pray. As we have seen, as we talk with God, we are overcome with the sense of our own futility and lowliness and yet at the same time we are excited because of the great honour He bestows on us! How marvellous that the God of the universe should be interested in hearing from us!

Elizabeth Clephane put it beautifully when she wrote:

> 'And from my smitten heart with tears,
> Two wonders I confess,
> The wonders of His glorious love
> And my own worthlessness.'

Prayer is co-operation with God

We are workers together with God (1 Corinthians 3:9). This, of course, covers many areas. When we preach or help the needy or demonstrate the fruit of the Spirit, we are clearly co-operating with the Lord. And we are obviously doing so when we pray. Indeed, prayer is one way in which even the humblest and most inadequate person can work with God. We may be able to do little else, but we can pray!

Geoffrey Bingham writes:

> 'Effective prayer is that prayer which is based upon a relationship with God, knowledge of His person and character, and most of all knowing the mind of God in relation to the purpose of His will . . .'[4]

Prayer is one area in which every believer can co-operate with God. No matter how much we may be limited by circumstances or health or inadequacy, we can always pray.

Men can pray. Women can pray. The elderly can pray. Children can pray. Academics can pray. The uneducated can pray. The sick and infirm can pray. Prisoners can pray. Soldiers can pray. Business people can pray. Labourers can pray. Clerks can pray. Politicians can pray. The lonely can pray. The despised and rejected can pray. The housebound can pray. Everyone can pray!

Prayer is a great privilege. We must never fall into the mistake of thinking that we have no need to pray. There are many reasons why prayer is essential for Christian living. Above all, we pray because through prayer we communicate with God. Nothing is more important than this.

Don't forget

- Hunger and thirst for God is the essence of true prayer.
- Prayer is a source of spiritual nourishment.
- Through prayer we draw spiritual strength.
- Through prayer we claim the blessings of God.
- Prayer is an act of obedience.
- Prayer pleases God.
- Prayer gives us a sense of dignity.
- Prayer is co-operation with God.

Notes

1   P. Billheimer, *Destined for the Throne* (CLC, 1975), p. 53.
2   Augustine of Hippo, *Confession*, I, 1.
3   G. Bingham, *Come Let Us Pray* (Blackwood: New Creation, 1988), p. 19.
4   ibid., p. 168.

Chapter 3

'On All Occasions'
(Ephesians 6:18)

Prayer in the Spirit is true prayer

We dare not pray if we do not pray in the Spirit. And to pray in the Spirit we must be filled with the Spirit. This sequence is clearly seen in Paul's letter to the Ephesians. First he says, *'Be filled with the Spirit'* (5:18) and then, *'Pray in the Spirit'* (6:18). In both cases, the Greek verbs have a sense of continuity. In other words, it is important to be filled with the Spirit all the time and it is important to pray in the Spirit all the time.

Not all prayer is prayer in the Spirit. At times, we may pray 'in the flesh'. In other words, we offer our invocations to God in our own efforts, rather than in the strength God's Spirit provides. This is obvious from Jesus' statement that true worshippers worship in Spirit and in truth (John 4:24). Clearly the reverse is also true: false worship is both fleshly and erroneous.

The same principles apply to prayer. True prayer is prayer in the Spirit and prayer in the Spirit is true prayer. This is, no doubt, the sort of thing James has in mind when he refers to people praying with wrong motives (James 4:3). Naturally, such prayers are not answered.

Praying in the Spirit is a marvellous form of communication with God in which our praying is impregnated by the life-giving presence and power of the Spirit of the Lord.

It is prayer **according to the will of God**, for the Spirit can only act ethically and with integrity.

It is **unselfish** prayer. The primary goal is the glory of Jesus and the unity of God's people.

It is also a **God-given** way of dealing with past hurts and wounds. While there is often a material or physical reason for our predicament, many times there are spiritual factors as well. And these can only be dealt with by the use of spiritual weapons.

The Bible names praying in the Holy Spirit as a primary part of the resources available to us in spiritual warfare. Having described the various items of Christian armour that believers need to wear – the breastplate of righteousness, the helmet of salvation, the shield of faith, the sword of the Spirit and so on – Paul then goes on to say:

> *'And pray in the Spirit on all occasions with all kinds of prayers and requests. With this in mind, be alert and always keep on praying for all the saints.'* (Ephesians 6:18)

This reflects the supreme priority of prayer in the life of the believer and the equally supreme priority of praying in the Spirit. Such praying is not an optional Christian extra. For example, Jesus forbade His disciples to begin their ministry until they were anointed by the Holy Spirit. And Paul makes it mandatory, with the imperative, *'Be filled with the Spirit'* (Ephesians 5:18). When we are Spirit-filled, our prayers will be, too.

There are many examples in history of the power of Spirit-anointed prayer. The great nineteenth-century American evangelist, D.L. Moody, wrote:

> 'I was crying all the time that God would fill me with his Holy Spirit. I can only say that God revealed himself to me and I had such an experience of his love that I had to ask him to stay his hand ... (Once) I was all the time tugging and carrying water. But now I have a river that carries me.' [1]

Congregationalist evangelist, Reuben Torrey, had a similar experience:

> 'One day as I sat in my study, something fell on me, and I literally fell to the floor, and I just lay there and shouted. I had never shouted before ... but I lay there shouting

"Glory to God! Glory to God! Glory to God!" ... The Spirit had put something in me that was not there before.' [2]

Such experiences are not just for those in professional ministry. In 1907, a Melbourne policeman named John Barclay wrote this:

'On Easter Monday evening, we all gathered ... for our usual praise and prayer meeting ... We all knelt down but no one seemed able to pray aloud. The only words I could utter were these: "Lord, reveal Thyself tonight." Presently, some mighty, marvelous unseen power took hold of me, and I was thrown face downwards on the floor, everything around me disappeared. The other friends were as if they never existed. I saw the heavens opened and my precious Jesus sitting on the throne. Oh, the joy and beauty and glory! It is unspeakable ... I was for about an hour and a half conscious only of the Lord's presence.

When I returned to earth again and looked around, some were kneeling in silent prayer, others were lying prostrate on the floor. Presently a sister broke out in prayer entreating God to bless His children and save lost souls. Then she prayed in a strange tongue ... and started singing in the same tongue. What heavenly music! ... I have never heard anything so sweet ... Our meeting lasted till four o'clock in the morning.' [3]

This is a dramatic illustration of the power of the Spirit in a prayer meeting. He does not always work so vividly. However, even when He moves quietly or non-dramatically, His presence is needed if we are to pray in the Spirit. There is a difference between ordinary prayer and prayer in the Spirit.

Not a matter of timing

It is not a matter of **timing** for we can pray in the Spirit 'on all occasions' (Ephesians 6:18). Praying is not just a Sunday activity or something we do in church, although it may, of course, include these. On the contrary, the Scripture urges us to pray continually (1 Thessalonians 5:17) and never to give up

(Luke 18:1). We can call upon God morning, noon and night (Psalm 55:17). His praises are to be in our mouths at all times (Psalm 34:1), both early and late (Psalm 92:2). Even in the middle of the night, we can commune with Him (Psalm 42:8).

Jesus prayed in the morning (Mark 1:35) and in the evening (Mark 6:46). At least once He prayed all night (Luke 6:12). He often withdrew to lonely places to pray (Luke 5:16).

We are urged to pray *'in the day of trouble'* (Psalm 50:15) as well as in the day of success (Acts 4:23–24).

In short, any time is a good time to pray in the Spirit. God neither slumbers nor sleeps (Psalm 121:3f.). His ear is always open to our prayers (Isaiah 59:1). But again, it must be authentic prayer. Sin will shut the ears of God (Isaiah 59:2).

As we walk in the Spirit, we can pray in the Spirit. This means a constant, ongoing fellowship with the Lord.

Not a matter of language

It is not the **language** of the prayer that makes it spiritual. There has been a tendency among charismatics to equate all prayer in the Spirit with the special prayer language of glossolalia or speaking in tongues. When Paul enjoins us to pray in the Spirit (Ephesians 6:18), however, he clearly includes praying in one's own language. He specifically names items for prayer which necessitate rational understanding and thought:

> *'And pray in the Spirit on all occasions with all kinds of prayers and requests. With this in mind, be alert and always keep on praying for all the saints. Pray also for me, that whenever I open my mouth, words may be given me so that I will fearlessly make known the mystery of the gospel, for which I am an ambassador in chains. Pray that I may declare it fearlessly, as I should.'*
> (Ephesians 6:18–20)

There is an emphasis here on being alert and awake; on remembering in prayer all the saints; on specifically upholding Paul and his ministry. This is intelligent praying – praying which is based on an informed understanding of particular needs. Epaphras is a fine example of this kind of ministry:

*'Epaphras, who is one of you and a servant of Christ Jesus, sends
greetings. He is always wrestling in prayer for you, that you may
stand firm in all the will of God, mature and fully assured.'*
(Colossians 4:12)

Note again the emphasis on Epaphras's commitment, dedication, earnestness and intelligence. He prays with great fervour,
but he also prays with knowledge. We may be sure he was also
praying in the Holy Spirit. He was clearly a Spirit-filled person
(Colossians 1:7–8; Philemon 23).

God does not disconnect our brains when we become disciples of Jesus. On the contrary, our minds are renewed and
we see things more clearly. Be transformed, says Paul, by the
renewing of your minds (Romans 12:1f.; Ephesians 4:23) and set
your minds on things above, where Christ is seated at God's
right hand (Colossians 3:1–3).

In his series of messages on the Sermon on the Mount, John
Wesley makes the following comment on Jesus' warning to us
not to *'use vain repetitions as the heathen do'*:

> 'Do not use abundance of words without any meaning. Say
> not the same thing over and over again; think not the fruit
> of your prayers depends on the length of them ... The
> thing here reproved is not simply the length, any more
> than the shortness, of our prayers ... First, length without
> meaning; speaking much, and meaning little or nothing;
> ... vain repetitions, as the Heathens did, reciting the names
> of their gods, over and over ... (or as some) Christians ...
> who say over and over the same string of prayers, without
> ever feeling what they speak ... Secondly, the thinking to
> be heard for our much speaking, the fancying God meas-
> ures prayers by their length, and is best pleased with those
> which contain the most words, which sound the longest in
> his ears. These are instances of superstition and folly.'

Praying in the Spirit means the discipline of rejecting unworthy
thoughts and focusing with deliberate intent on the things of
God. In Colossians 3, Paul uses two strong imperative verbs.
Firstly, he says 'seek' or 'be zealous for' things above (3:1). Then
he tells us to 'set our minds' on these as well (3:2). There is an

obvious sequence here. First, the motivation, then the action. If we are enthusiastic, we will last the distance. Disciplined thinking without fervour of spirit is not easy. On the other hand, zeal for God should lead to disciplined minds.

> *'For God did not give us a spirit of timidity, but a spirit of power, of love and of self-discipline.'*   (2 Timothy 1:7)

So God expects us to think when we pray. Jesus often appealed to people's understanding (Matthew 16:9, 11; 24:43; John 13:12) and urged them to think things through (Matthew 17:25; 18:12; 21:28; Luke 10:36). So it is necessary for us to pray wisely and thoughtfully and to discipline our thinking so it is under the Spirit's control.

Peter puts it as plainly as possible:

> *'The end of all things is near. Therefore be clear minded and self-controlled so that you can pray . . . you are blessed, for the Spirit of glory and of God rests on you.'*   (1 Peter 4:7, 14)

Admittedly, there is a gap of seven verses between the reference to thoughtful prayer and the Spirit of glory, but the connection is still valid. The point is that to pray in the Spirit in no way negates the use of the mind. On the contrary, we pray in Spirit and in truth, blending the two in a godly balance. When we pray, we need to bring our thinking into line with the Word of God and monitor our thinking so that we pray wisely and well.

This is not to say that spiritual praying does not include praying in tongues. As we shall see, later, when the Holy Spirit infuses our prayers, it is often by giving us a new prayer-language. But it is to say that the Holy Spirit is above language. So Paul writes,

> *'I will pray with my spirit* [that is, in an unknown tongue], *but I will also pray with my mind; I will sing with my spirit, but I will also sing with my mind.'*   (1 Corinthians 14:15)

Whether we speak in our own tongue or one He gives us, we can still pray in the Spirit. The important thing is not what language we are able to use but to what extent the Spirit is able to use us.

Don't forget

- When we are Spirit-filled, our prayers will be, too.
- It is not a matter of timing for we can pray in the Spirit 'on all occasions'.
- It is not a matter of language but of allowing the Holy Spirit to infuse our prayers with Himself.

Notes

1   J.C. Pollock, *Moody Without Sankey* (London: Hodder and Stoughton, 1963), p. 87.
2   *The Torrey-Alexander Souvenir* (1902), p. 77.
3   M.W. Moorhead, *A Cloud of Witnesses to Pentecost in India*, Pamphlet No. 4 (Bombay 1908).

Chapter 4

'With All Kinds of Prayers'
(Ephesians 6:18)

Not form, but attitude

Paul tells us to pray on all occasions with every kind of prayer and request in the Spirit (Ephesians 6:18).

This is a great encouragement to us to bring all our needs to God no matter what they are. Every prayer and request is to be raised before God's throne. Elsewhere, Paul urges us to present our petitions and requests to God in everything (Philippians 4:6) and the writer to the Hebrews says,

> *'Let us then approach the throne of grace with confidence, so that we may receive mercy and find grace to help us in our time of need.'* (Hebrews 4:16)

These statements all encourage us to believe that any kind of prayer is acceptable to God if we come to Him in Christ.

Not a matter of form

The **form** of prayer is not critical. Praying may be both spontaneous or liturgical. It may arise from the overflowing of the heart in a loving, joyful response to the bountiful grace of God. Or it may express itself in a learned petition or a read orison.

It is a matter of mind, emotion and will. We pray intelligently, we pray feelingly and we pray deliberately. Our whole personalities are involved.

True praying touches the affections. The great eighteenth-century revivalist and philosopher Jonathan Edwards put it graphically when he wrote:

> 'Nothing is more manifest in fact, than that the things of religion take hold of men's souls no further than they affect them ... I am bold to assert that there never was any considerable change wrought in the mind or conversation of any person, by anything of a religious nature that ever he read, heard or saw, that had not his affections moved.' [1]

It is often argued that it is dangerous to base one's faith on feelings. And this is true enough. Emotions are notoriously fickle. But they are also real. A faith that never feels anything is no faith at all. How can we be in communion with the heavenly Father and not feel loved and cared for and valued? How can we contemplate the depths of Christ's love in His atoning sacrifice on the cross and not be moved? How can we accept the superb reality of the resurrection and not feel like shouting for joy?

This means that prayer in the Spirit may include weeping, yearning or even laughter. There is a refreshing that comes from petitions encased in tears. There is spiritual reinvigoration in worship that rises in holy laughter and joy.

Many Spirit-filled Christians like to pray extemporaneous prayers, using their own words and phrases. However, there is also a place for structured praying. Many of the greatest prayers have been thoughtfully prepared, written down and repeated over and again by thousands of Christians. One of the best known is:

> 'Lord, grant me the courage to change the things I can,
> the serenity to accept the things I can't,
> and the wisdom to know the difference.'

Then there is the famous prayer of Francis of Assisi:

> 'Lord, make me an instrument of thy peace.
> Where there is hatred, let me sow love;
>   where there is injury, pardon;
>   where there is doubt, faith;

where there is despair, hope;
where there is darkness, light;
where there is sadness, joy.
O divine Master, grant that I may seek,
    not so much to be consoled,
    as to console;
    not so much to be understood,
    as to understand;
    not so much to be loved,
    as to love.
For it is in giving that we receive;
    it is in pardoning that we are pardoned;
    it is in dying that we awaken to eternal life.'

Such a prayer can be prayed in the flesh, of course, by the mere repetition of the words. But it can also be a prayer in the Spirit, raised to God with sincerity and truth. In fact, sometimes it is easier to pray such a prayer with fervour than one of our own composition.

On the other hand, simple words are often the best. What would you think if your teenage son came to you saying, 'O great and awesome Father, I humbly beseech thee to vouchsafe your humble child two dollars for a Coke...'?

There is a story of a young minister who, trying to impress his new congregation, began his opening prayer with words like these: 'Almighty, omnipotent, omniscient, beneficent Creator and Lord of the Universe ... What shall we call Thee?' An old saint in the front row interjected, 'Call Him Father, sonny!' Which, of course, is just what Jesus told us to do! *'When you pray, say: "Father..."'* (Luke 11:4).

Not a matter of posture

Some people like to kneel when they pray. This is a traditional prayer stance and it's a good one, because it expresses our sense of awe in the presence of God. In some churches, kneeling rails are provided to make it easier to bow before the Lord.

Kneeling is a biblical prayer pose. *'Let us kneel before the* Lord *our Maker,'* cries the psalmist, *'for he is God'* (Psalm 95:6–7). Jesus knelt to pray in Gethsemane (Luke 22:41). Stephen fell on his knees as he prayed the last prayer of his life (Acts 7:60) and Peter knelt when he called on God for the restoration of Dorcas (Acts 9:40). On two occasions it is recorded that Paul knelt with other believers to pray (Acts 20:36; 21:5) and he sometimes refers to kneeling as a favoured prayer posture (e.g. Ephesians 3:14). Kneeling is an indication of homage to someone greater than we are. So in mock-prayer, the soldiers bowed before Jesus (Matthew 27:29). Of course, the day is also coming when every human being will kneel before God (Isaiah 45:23; Philippians 2:10).

Sadly, some Protestants have rejected kneeling because of ancient associations with kneeling at the altar. This is a pity because kneeling is a sound, biblical position to adopt.

But we also read in Scripture of other postures for prayer – standing (1 Kings 8:14), sitting (Acts 2:2), bowing (Psalm 95:6), lying in bed (Psalm 63:6), lifting hands (1 Timothy 2:8), walking (Psalm 89:15), lifting one's eyes (John 17:1), falling prostrate (Nehemiah 8:6).

I remember a men's camp where at one point all present were lying face down on the floor, their arms spread before them, in worship and humility. It was a moving and memorable occasion.

Sometimes, in biblical days, people prayed in silence (Psalm 46:10; Habakkuk 2:20; Zephaniah 1:7); sometimes they sang and shouted (Psalms 81:1; 95:1); sometimes they clapped their hands (Psalms 47:1; 98:8); sometimes they played tambourines and blew trumpets (Psalms 149 and 150)!

The posture is not crucial. At different times, we may feel the need to adopt different positions. What is important is being in the Spirit. It is significant that the apostles were seated when they were filled with the Holy Spirit at Pentecost (Acts 2:2).

For many years, I used to walk our dog in the mornings. I was able to do three things at once – exercise my body, exercise the dog and exercise my soul in prayer. We no longer have a dog, but I am still able to walk and talk with the Lord. In fact, this is my favourite way of praying. I love to commune with God like this. And it also prevents me from being distracted by books or papers on my desk or other members of the family.

Somebody once wrote a few simple lines that clearly emphasize that it is attitude, not position, which matters:

'*Attitudes in Prayer*
"The proper way for man to pray,"
Said Rev Dr Keys,
"The proper attitude in prayer,
Is down upon one's knees."

"No, I should say the way to pray,"
Said old Professor Wise,
"Is standing straight,
With outstretched arms,
And rapturous, upturned eyes."

"It seems to me the hands should be
Devoutly clasped in front,
With both thumbs pointing to the ground,"
Said Rev Samuel Blunt.

"Last year I fell in 'Odgkins' well head-first,"
Said Ocker Brown,
"With both me 'eels a-stickin' up,
Me 'ead was pointin' down.

"I prayed a prayer right then and there,
Best prayer I ever said.
The greatest prayer I ever prayed
Was standin' on me 'ead!" '

Wherever we are is a good place to pray if the Spirit is there
with us. Indeed, in one sense, there is nowhere we can go
without God's Spirit. David puts it graphically in a well-known
psalm:

'*Where can I go from your Spirit?*
   Where can I flee from your presence?
If I go up to the heavens, you are there;
   if I make my bed in the depths, you are there.
If I rise on the wings of the dawn,
   if I settle on the far side of the sea,
even there your hand will guide me,
   your right hand will hold me fast.'   (Psalm 139:7–10)

Pray to get an answer

The verses quoted above tell us something else about prayer. It's also a matter of attitude. There's no doubt that desperation adds greatly to the effectiveness of our praying.

Jesus taught this in one of His parables. When, urgently in need of bread, you go to your neighbour in the middle of the night, He said, he gives it to you, not because you are his friend, but because you make such a nuisance of yourself that he wants to get rid of you so he can go back to bed (Luke 11:5–8)!

It is because of your 'boldness', says Jesus, that you get what you want.

Not that we should be proud or irreverent, of course. But maybe we need to rethink our concept of reverence. It is usually associated with silence, dignity, shyness, hesitancy and the like. Until the last few decades, most church buildings have been erected to reinforce this concept. They are designed to intimidate. The architecture carries a message – God is great and we are small. We must not sneeze or cough or speak or drop anything because, if we do, it will be heard by everyone else. Every misdemeanour is magnified as it echoes around the building. We are almost frightened to breathe.

Of course, God **is** great and we **are** small. But this should not intimidate us. Jesus makes it plain in this parable. Because we are not hindered by an exaggerated sense of reverence, we hammer on the neighbour's door with 'brazen insistence' until we get what we want. Similarly, it is when we pray with persistence and determination that our prayers are answered.

Does this mean that we must twist God's arm before He will act? No. But it does mean we need to be serious about prayer. We need to be willing to give ourselves to it with commitment and steadfastness. It is our attitude that makes the difference. Like Jacob, we will not let go of God until He blesses us (Genesis 32:26)!

This does not necessarily mean long prayers. When you are upside down in a well, your prayers are necessarily short. But it does mean determined prayers. It means claiming the promises of God with such desperate tenacity that we will not stop until He responds. In fact, some have suggested that Jesus' parable actually encourages us to be 'cheeky' when we approach God.

Such an idea is abhorrent to many people, of course. But perhaps it is not so far from the truth. Jesus told us that we need to approach God like little children (Matthew 18:4) and that the kingdom of heaven belongs to those who are like them (Matthew 19:14). Might not the Lord be pleased when we approach Him in simple, child-like faith, not always observing the niceties of good manners, but loving Him and delighting to receive good things from Him? Might He not be pleased when we are determined to draw upon the treasures of His bounty?

In another parable, Jesus spoke of a widow who so pestered a judge that he finally gave in (Luke 18:1ff.). It was because she kept 'bothering' him that he yielded. Jesus told this parable to teach us that we should *'pray and not give up'* (Luke 18:1). He went on to say:

> *'And will not God bring about justice for his chosen ones, who cry out to him day and night? Will he keep putting them off? I tell you, he will see that they get justice, and quickly.'*
>
> (Luke 18:7–8a)

But He then went on to raise an interesting question,

> *'However, when the Son of Man comes, will he find faith on the earth?'*   (Luke 18:8b)

Why should He say this at this point? Clearly, there is a correlation between determination and faith. Determination on its own is not enough. It must be grounded in faith before it will achieve results. Without faith, the scripture says, it is impossible to please God (Hebrews 11:6). We would like to say, 'Without faith it is difficult to please God.' But this is not what the Bible says. Faith is an absolute essential, a *sine qua non* – a quality without which nothing can be achieved.

But when we do pray in faith, with persistence, anything can happen.

A matter of Spirit

To pray in the Spirit is not difficult. It is simply a matter of tapping into God's presence and power and staying there. It is not a matter of language or form or posture. It is a matter of being filled with the Spirit and praying in the strength and power He offers.

Then, wherever we are, we can truly pray on all occasions with all kinds of prayer in the Spirit!

Don't forget

- Prayer in the Spirit involves the whole personality.
- Prayer in the Spirit involves the mind, the emotions and the will.
- Prayer in the Spirit may be extemporaneous or structured.
- Prayer in the Spirit is not a matter of posture or place.
- Prayer in the Spirit is dependent on attitude.
- Wherever we are is a good place to pray.

Note

1   Jonathan Edwards, *The Religious Affections* (Edinburgh: The Banner of Truth Trust, [1746] 1984), p. 30.

Chapter 5

Requests, Prayers, Intercessions and Thanksgivings
(Ephesians 6:18)

Whether it be prayer or praise,
asking or thanking, communing or worshipping –
it all needs to be in the Spirit

There is no single form of prayer which is identifiable as prayer in the Spirit. This is obvious from Paul's injunction to us to *'pray in the Spirit on all occasions with all kinds of prayers and requests'* (Ephesians 6:18). Whether it is prayer or praise, asking or thanking, communing or worshipping – it all needs to be in the Spirit.

Prayer

For prayer itself, as commonly understood, several different words are used in the New Testament. The first, and most common, is *proseuchomai* which simply means to 'pray'. It occurs 90 times in 82 verses in the New Testament.

From this verb comes the common noun *proseuche* which means 'prayer' and occurs 37 times in 37 verses (e.g. Matthew 17:21; Acts 1:14; 2:42; 10:31; Ephesians 6:18; Philippians 4:6; Colossians 4:2; James 5:17; Revelation 5:8; 8:3, 4).

This word group was commonly used in Greek for any kind of prayer to any god. Christians used the same word to describe talking with the true God – and only with Him.[1] It is a general term and really covers every form of prayer. But it also describes communion with God. So it has special reference to conversational prayer when we just chat with the Lord, as it were, and enjoy His company.

This kind of praying can be as much in the Spirit as any other kind. It is by the Spirit that we enjoy close communion with God who makes us one Spirit with Him (1 Corinthians 6:17).

In fact, one of the most natural forms of praying is simply to hold a conversation with God. There are some beautiful bushland and water scenes near where we live and as I walk and talk with the Lord, I often find myself saying things like, 'Father, you did a wonderful job with that blue-water bay. And that white-barked ghost gum tree – it's magnificent!' When my wife, Vanessa, and I walk together it is sometimes a three-way conversation.

Jesus used the common word for prayer in His teaching in the Sermon on the Mount (Matthew 5:44; 6:5, 6, 7, 9; 14:23). It is used for His own praying in the Garden of Gethsemane (Matthew 26:36, 39, 41, 42, 44); for the prayers of the apostles (Acts 1:24; 8:15; 13:3) and those of the early Church (1 Corinthians 11:4, 5, 13); for praying in tongues (1 Corinthians 14:13, 14, 15); and for praying in the Spirit (Ephesians 6:18; 1 Thessalonians 5:17, 25; James 5:13, 14, 17, 18; Jude 20).

Asking

Another common term is *deesis* which is translated as 'petition', 'request' or 'supplication'. It is found 19 times in 17 verses.

This word was commonly used in New Testament times of petitions to superiors such as kings or rulers and hence was applied specifically to requests made to God in prayer.[2]

So Paul urges that such petitions be made for political leaders (1 Timothy 2:1) and James links it with prayer for the sick (James 5:16). Paul's earnest prayer for the salvation of Israel is a *deesis* (Romans 10:1). And to the Philippians, he advocates using both prayers and petitions in every situation (Philippians 4:6, 7).

Then there is *enteuxis* which also means 'prayer' or 'petition'. It only occurs twice in the New Testament, both times in Paul's first letter to Timothy (2:1; 4:5). The verb form is also used – but only of Christ (Hebrews 7:25) and the Holy Spirit (Romans 8:26, 27) interceding for us.

Another less common term is *aitema* which means 'request'. It is used especially in the context of answered prayer – when we make such requests, in faith, the answer is always forthcoming (Philippians 4:6; 1 John 5:15)! This is related to the more common verb *aiteo* which simply means to 'ask'. So Jesus tells us to ask in order that we might receive (Luke 11:9ff.) and John promises that we can ask in confidence when we ask according to God's will (1 John 5:14). In fact, the Lord tells us over and over again to ask in prayer so that God can act on our behalf (John 14:14; 15:7; 15:16) and rebukes His disciples for not asking for enough (John 16:24)! He puts it very plainly when He says,

> *'Until now you have not asked for anything in my name. Ask and you will receive, and your joy will be complete.'*
> (John 16:24)

He could hardly be more encouraging. 'Ask!' He says. 'So far, you haven't been asking enough. But if you do ask, you will receive. Why be sad when by asking you can experience fullness of joy?'

Some people are afraid we might ask God for too much. Jesus seemed more concerned that we might not ask for enough. For example, how many times did He rebuke His disciples for trying to use too much faith? Yet many times He chastised them for having too little! When the disciples were caught in a storm at sea, He said, *'You of little faith, why are you so afraid?'* (Matthew 8:26). He made a similar remark to Peter, *'You of little faith, why did you doubt?'* (Matthew 14:31). Later, He rebuked the disciples for fearing that God might not provide their needs (Matthew 16:8). When they asked Him why they couldn't help an epileptic boy, He replied, *'Because you have so little faith'* (Matthew 17:20). In the Sermon on the Mount He urged people to trust God for food and clothing and to have more faith (Luke 12:28). After the resurrection, He rebuked the disciples for *'their stubborn refusal to believe'* (Mark 16:14). He spoke sternly to the two men on the road to Emmaus – *'How foolish you are and how slow of heart to believe!'* He said (Luke 24:25).

There is no doubt that Jesus was frequently disappointed by people's failure to show more faith. Over and again, He urged His followers to ask and to ask in faith. The same situation occurs today. Most of the time our problem is that we ask, not for too much, but for too little. Through prayer, we learn how to ask from God.

Of course, not everything we want is the will of God. We are often foolish in our asking. But there are scores of things that plainly **are** the will of God for us – and these we **can** ask for. Forgiveness is an obvious example. Deliverance from Satan and his hosts is another. Then there is:

- victory over temptation
- peace of heart
- reconciliation with our enemies
- guidance
- freedom from depression
- freedom from care
- more love in our lives
- more patience
- more gentleness
- more humility
- more grace
- more courage.

We can ask for:

- the fullness of the Holy Spirit
- spiritual gifts
- daily bread
- our basic needs to be met
- the Word of God to dwell in our hearts
- strength in difficult times
- joy in the midst of sadness
- light in periods of gloom
- self-control in the way we live.

All of these are promised to us in Scripture. There are dozens of others.

Do we ever really ask for enough? Asking is a significant aspect of praying and we ought not to hold back too much. Jesus said, *'whatever you ask for in prayer, believe that you have received it, and it will be yours'* (Mark 11:24).

There are several places where two or more of these terms are used together (Ephesians 6:18; Philippians 4:6; 1 Timothy 2:1).

The strongest teaching on asking is given by the Lord Jesus Himself:

> *'Suppose one of you has a friend, and he goes to him at midnight and says, "Friend, lend me three loaves of bread, because a friend of mine on a journey has come to me, and I have nothing to set before him."*
>
> *Then the one inside answers, "Don't bother me. The door is already locked, and my children are with me in bed. I can't get up and give you anything." I tell you, though he will not get up and give him the bread because he is his friend, yet because of the man's boldness he will get up and give him as much as he needs.*
>
> *So I say to you: Ask and it will be given to you; seek and you will find; knock and the door will be opened to you. For everyone who asks receives; he who seeks finds; and to him who knocks, the door will be opened.*
>
> *Which of you fathers, if your son asks for a fish, will give him a snake instead? Or if he asks for an egg, will give him a scorpion? If you then, though you are evil, know how to give good gifts to your children, how much more will your Father in heaven give the Holy Spirit to those who ask him!'*
>
> (Luke 11:5–13)

In this parable, Jesus emphasizes the value of persistence when we ask God for something in prayer. In earthly relationships, people are not put off by delay or a first refusal when asking of a true friend. If their desire is deep enough they will persist faithfully, particularly if they have confidence in their friend's ability to give. So we, too, need to continue in prayer without giving up (Luke 18:1).

Jesus describes three aspects of prayer:

- ask – articulate, i.e. define the need
- seek – attitude, i.e. persistence
- knock – action, i.e. doing something about it.

Too often, we stop at asking, without seeking or knocking. We need to realize the importance of continuing to seek God in prayer. The fact is that a dogged persistence often reveals the depth of our commitment to our requests.

The word 'boldness' used here is interesting. It is a translation of the Greek *aneideia* which has connotations of boldness, importunity, shameless persistency or impudence. Jesus commends praying in this fashion. The opposite is *aidos* which means 'bashfulness', 'modesty', 'awe', 'reverence'. Ironically, these are the qualities we have been taught for years that we should express in prayer! For centuries, Christians have been instructed to be 'reverent' and non-assertive in approaching God. We have been warned against presumption or taking the promises of Scripture too literally. It's all right to ask God for things, but we mustn't be surprised if we don't get them. We certainly shouldn't make any demands of God. While there is undoubtedly some truth in all this, Jesus tells us to take an entirely opposite attitude!

When we come to God asking for His blessing, we must not give up. We can be truly encouraged by the fact that just as an earthly parent will only give good food to a child, so will our heavenly Father only give good things – especially the Holy Spirit – to us (Luke 11:11–13). There is no danger of the devil slipping in with a substitute or counterfeit answer. If we ask God, it is God who responds; Jesus assures us of this. God is good (Ezra 3:11; Psalms 136:1; 145:9; Romans 8:28)!

Ultimately, our faith is based on the goodness of God. Because He is good, we can trust Him to answer prayer and to honour our faith at all times, according to His promise in the best possible way! All the promises of God are 'Yes' and 'Amen' in Christ (2 Corinthians 1:20). Christ is God's guarantee that all His promises are reliable.

Intercession

What is interesting is that one of our most common words for prayer today is rarely used in the New Testament. This is the word 'intercession'. Strangely enough, this term is never applied to believers. When it is applied in a prayer context, it is always only of Christ or the Holy Spirit. (The word translated 'intercessions' in 1 Timothy 2:1 is *deesis*.)

The Greek word is *entugchano* which means to 'plead, appeal or turn to God on behalf of another'. The word is based on the idea of going to meet someone to present a case to him. This may be in favour of another person – but it may also be against him. In this sense it can mean to accuse or complain about someone.[3] The Jews, for example, went to Festus to ask him to do something about Paul (Acts 25:24) and Paul recalls how Elijah *'appealed to God against Israel'* (Romans 11:2). Elsewhere in the New Testament, however, the verb is used only of Jesus or the Holy Spirit, and therefore means to 'appeal positively on behalf of others'.

In fact, the way in which *entugchano* is used in the New Testament indicates it means more than this. To intercede is not just to pray a prayer: it is to act as a bridge or a go-between. In this sense, only Jesus can truly intercede. He *'always lives to intercede'* for us (Hebrews 7:25). He is able to do this, because He died for us and rose again. By His death He earned the right to speak on our behalf; by His life, He is able to do so forever.

In this sense, He always stands between us and God, an eternal intercessor. This does not mean He is actually praying for us as such. But in His person, He provides a way through to God.

In Old Testament days, Moses is an outstanding example of one who interceded for His people (Exodus 32:31–32; Psalm 106:23). Not only did he pray for them, but he offered his life for them. Then there are several Old Testament passages that deplore the lack of intercessors (Isaiah 59:16; 63:5; 64:7; Ezekiel 22:30). Now this lack has been eternally met in Christ.

So, technically, it is an incorrect use of scriptural language to talk of believers interceding for one another. This is a unique ministry of Jesus. Paul realized this. He wanted to be an intercessor for his people – but not just in praying for them.

He would have sacrificed his life for them if he could (Romans 9:1–5). And this is what intercession really means. It is not just praying or speaking up on behalf of another. It is actually being a go-between.

Of course, there is a pressing need for believers to pray for one another. Frequently the New Testament writers urge us to mutual prayer. Paul pleads:

> *'pray for us that God may open a door for our message, so that we may proclaim the mystery of Christ, for which I am in chains. Pray that I may proclaim it clearly, as I should.'*
> (Colossians 4:3–4; cf. Ephesians 6:19–20)

Again and again, he writes, 'Pray for us' (Romans 15:30; Colossians 4:18; 1 Thessalonians 5:25; Philemon 22). James, too, urges us to pray for one another that we may be healed (James 5:16).

Indeed, from the New Testament we can form quite a list of people we should pray for:

- *'everyone'* (1 Timothy 2:1)
- kings (1 Timothy 2:2)
- all in authority (1 Timothy 2:2)
- all the saints (Romans 8:27; Ephesians 6:18)
- one another (James 5:16)
- our city (Jeremiah 29:7)
- our nation (Exodus 32:31, 32)
- missionaries (Ephesians 6:19; Colossians 4:3).

Obviously, this list could be expanded further. But even as it is, there is enough to keep us busy for a long time!

Don't forget

- Our problem is that we ask for too little, not that we ask for too much.
- Through prayer we learn how to ask from God.

- Because God is good we can trust Him to answer prayer.
- There is an urgent need for believers to pray for one another.
- Prayer in the Spirit is a serious encounter with God.

Notes

1   J. Moulton and G. Milligan, *The Vocabulary of the Greek New Testament* (London: Hodder and Stoughton, 1963), p. 547.

2   ibid., p. 137; F. Rienecker, *A Linguistic Key to the Greek New Testament* (Grand Rapids: Regency (Zondervan) 1980), pp. 618f.

3   W.J. Perschbacher (ed.), *The New Analytical Greek Lexicon* (Peabody, Mass.: Hendrickson,1990), p. 146; Rienecker, *A Linguistic Key to the Greek New Testament*.

Chapter 6

'Join Me in My Struggle
by Praying to God for Me'
(Romans 15:30)

*Through praying for people regularly,
we develop a 'fellowship of prayer'*

Some years ago, Robert Colman, singer, worship leader and a
pastor friend of mine, said to me, 'You know that Carol and I
pray for you and Vanessa every Saturday morning.'

'Do you? Really?' I replied in astonishment. If they had been
really close friends I might have been less surprised. But Robert
and Carol live a thousand kilometres from us and we rarely see
them.

'Yes,' he replied with a smile. 'We really do.'

I was challenged by this because Vanessa and I were not
praying for them. So I resolved to rectify this and made a
practice of remembering them regularly before God. Once I
began doing this I thought of other friends in the ministry who
also merited prayer. So I began to compile a list. Slowly it grew
until there were dozens of names. Then I added friends who
were not in the ministry. And then students whom I taught and
colleagues and board members and family. Eventually I developed a diary in which I had lists of names for each day of the
week. Monday – family and friends; Tuesday – colleagues;
Wednesday – College graduates; Thursday – ministerial associates; Friday – my own life and work; Saturday – politicians and
church leaders; Sunday – the church where I would be worshipping or ministering that day.

This has become a pattern of prayer that has given strength and discipline to my spiritual life. But there has also been another benefit. One that might be called the 'fellowship of prayer'. I have discovered that by praying regularly for people like this, I feel I know them better, even people whom I never see. Through naming them before God on a regular basis – and that is often all I do – they become more real, more warm, more part of my life.

There is no doubt that the Scripture enjoins us to pray for one another. To quote Ephesians 6:18 again, *'always keep on praying for all the saints.'* It is easy to do this in a general sense. But naming people individually gives infinitely greater meaning to such prayers. When we lift people one by one before the Lord, a deepening and meaningful fellowship of grace and love develops. It enables us to know and appreciate one another better. We may not actually be in the same place as them, but it seems as if we are. Perhaps Paul had something like this in mind when he told the Corinthians that his spirit was present with them (1 Corinthians 5:3).

Certainly, the throne of grace is one place where we can all meet. Even though we may be separated geographically and perhaps by language or culture or denomination, we find a common meeting point before God. No matter who we are or what our differences, when we pray there is only one place we can go. Here is a place of true unity and fellowship.

But there is more to praying for one another than fellowship. In his letter to the Romans Paul makes a remarkable request:

> *'I urge you, brothers, by our Lord Jesus Christ and by the love of the Spirit, to join me in my struggle by praying to God for me. Pray that I may be rescued from the unbelievers in Judea and that my service in Jerusalem may be acceptable to the saints there, so that by God's will I may come to you with joy and together with you be refreshed. The God of peace be with you all. Amen.'* (Romans 15:30–33)

What catches our attention here is the phrase *'join me in my struggle by praying to God for me.'* The implications of this request are more than meet the eye. The point the apostle is making to the Roman Christians is that by praying for him they were actually taking part in his ministry. Although they were not there with him, they were still helping him in his work.

This is a profound and encouraging insight. It means that when we pray for others – especially others in ministry – it is as if we were there with them in their work. We may not be able to travel interstate or overseas, to traverse the oceans, cross the nation or even drive across the city – but even so, we can be with them by praying for them. We can actually be part of their work.

To put it another way, even people who are not missionaries can be missionaries. We may not in fact trudge through jungles or pick our way through slums or preach in the villages or proclaim the gospel or organize rallies or minister to the sick or distribute Bibles or set up schools or plant churches. But through praying for those who do these things we are spiritually there all the same.

We may not be on hand when distant friends or loved ones are suffering ill health or family pressures of marital stress or unemployment or unfair criticism or financial problems or spiritual battles – but through praying for them we are in a sense present with them after all.

In spite of all we can say about prayer, there are always some mysteries. This is one of them. How can we be part of another's struggle by praying for them? Ultimately, only God knows. But we ourselves can experience a glimpse of it. When we pray, there is no doubt we grow more aware of the challenges others are facing. We feel more conscious of the difficulties and needs they experience. We can even sense something of the pain, heartache and stress they undergo.

But it is more than this. In some wonderful, divinely ordained way, we actually help them in what they are doing. When we pray for one another we help one another. When we fail to pray, that help languishes. Perhaps this is one reason why the prophet Samuel called failure to pray for one another a sin (1 Samuel 12:23).

Prayer in the Spirit means wrestling in prayer

The term Paul employs here is a strong one. He uses the Greek compound verb *sunagonidzomai*. The prefix *sun* means 'together' and has come into many English words in the form 'syn-' or 'sym-'. Obvious examples are nouns such as 'synagogue', a place where people gather together, and 'symphony', music where sounds are combined together. The primary root (*agonidzomai*) means to contend or fight or strive earnestly. Obviously, it is from this word that we derive the English words 'agonize' and 'agony'. The compound verb is a technical term that might be used about an athletic contest in which two people are striving together, even to the point of pain, to win the event. It might also apply to pursuing a law suit or being engaged in a stage show.[1] So to pray for another person is to act like this – to use all one's energy and effort to struggle on to victory. It is not quite 'agonizing' in prayer, but it is certainly praying with passion and determination.

Note how Paul introduces his request with two qualifiers. It is through the Lord Jesus Christ and through the love of the Spirit that we pray like this. These are critical requirements. First, it is only through Christ that we can pray any prayer. If we do not come through Him, we cannot come at all. This may seem a strong statement. Surely God answers prayers even if they are not prayed in Jesus' name – as He did with Cornelius, for example (Acts 10:30ff.). Yes, but in such cases, it is clear that failure to pray in Christ's name was not by design, but through ignorance. The Scripture makes it very plain that it is *'his name through faith in his name'* (Acts 3:16 AV) that brings answers to prayer. Jesus Himself told us to pray in His name (John 14:13; 16:24). When we pray in His name, we know the Father hears us.

Second, it is *'by the love of the Spirit'* that we pray successfully. The Holy Spirit is the one who enables us to pray effectively. We don't know how to pray as we should but the Spirit helps us to do it (Romans 8:26f.). One way in which He helps us is by filling our hearts with love. This love is then the motivator for our prayers. We join others in their struggle because the Spirit enables us to love them sufficiently to do so. The love of God is poured into our hearts by the Holy Spirit (Romans 5:5) and the first fruit of the Holy Spirit is love (Galatians 5:22).

Perhaps the first step in enhancing our prayers for others is to ask the Holy Spirit to bless us with a greater love. Out of this love will then grow a concern for others and from this concern will come effective and active prayers.

Joining people in their struggle through prayer requires love.
For it means not just a casual, 'God bless Anthony' or, 'Lord, be
with Naomi.' It means spending time before God pouring out
our hearts in deep and caring concern. It means feeling the pain
of those we pray for. It means entering their world, as it were,
and somehow participating in their experience.

This is where the Spirit's help is so crucial. For our own
understanding and knowledge is so limited, but the Spirit can
reveal to us the matters that need our attention. With a spirit of
wisdom and revelation, we can pray with intelligence and
accuracy. We may not have any human knowledge of the
struggle others are facing, but we may have a spiritual concern.

How this works out in practice is more sensed than understood. We may not have an intellectual understanding of the
situation concerned. But we may well have a deep sense of
urgency or compassion or even desperation that will drive us to
passionate prayer. Years ago, people used to talk about having a
'burden' in prayer. By this they meant they actually experienced
a kind of heavy weight upon them as they prayed and they
could not desist until the weight lifted. It is almost a physical
sensation – a divine pressure that gently yet strongly holds us in
prayer until the needs are met. Then comes a kind of release, a
sense of liberation that the hour is passed and we can now relax.

It is obvious that praying in tongues is virtually essential here.
When we don't know the details of people's struggles, we are
utterly dependent on the Holy Spirit to give us the words with
which to pray. When we pray in a tongue, we make intercession
fluently and powerfully according to the will of God. Person-
ally, I don't know how I would cope if it were not for this prayer
gift. It is only by Spirit-enabled prayer like this that we can
sustain extended times of labouring before God as we join in
the struggle of others.

So Paul reminds us that when we pray in tongues we speak
divine secrets or mysteries (1 Corinthians 14:2) and that it is not
the mind, but the spirit which prays (1 Corinthians 14:14).

Epaphras – a model for prayer

Epaphras is a challenging model for prayer. It was he who
founded the church at Colossae. Later he visited Paul in Rome.

In his letter to the Colossians, Paul reminded them that Epaphras was *'always wrestling in prayer'* for them (4:12). The same verb is used here as in Romans 15:30. Because of his love and concern for the church he founded, Epaphras could not just ignore them or forget them. He was no longer there with them, but their concerns were still his and their needs were as heavy upon him as ever. There were none of the instant communication methods we can employ today. He couldn't make a phone call or send an email. He couldn't even pay them a quick visit to see how they were doing. There was nothing practical he could do to help them. So he did the one thing he could do – he wrestled before God for them in prayer. He knew how to join his people in their struggle.

Like him, we can wrestle in prayer for our brothers and sisters (Colossians 4:12). To 'agonize' in prayer is to throw everything into it, to pray earnestly and sincerely and passionately, to pray to the best of our ability. Not only did Epaphras pray like this, but he did it *'always'*. It was not a flash in the pan, some momentary burst of prayer arising from an exciting meeting or an emotional experience of some kind. It was a pattern of life for him. The word 'always' means the same in Greek as it does in English. The model Epaphras presents us is of a man who did not give up easily; a man who could pray regularly and continually and steadfastly for those he loved; a man who understood the dynamics of joining together spiritually in prayer with people from whom he was separated physically in practice.

It is also interesting to see why he wrestled in prayer for them – that they might *'stand firm in all the will of God, mature and fully assured'* (Colossians 4:12).

When we pray today it is easy for us to pray for more obvious but more trivial things. We are so dominated by the physical and the material, we tend to pray for these needs. What Epaphras prayed for was that the Colossians might *'stand firm in all the will of God'*. What a wonderful prayer. It encompasses everything. He did not just pray that those people would do God's will, but that they would stand firm in *'all'* of it. If we can succeed in this we can succeed in anything. When we stand firm in all God's will, it naturally follows that we avoid sin, overcome evil, live godly lives, love one another, display the gifts and fruit of the Holy Spirit and generally please God.

I know that I greatly value people praying like this for me! I need such prayers. I want to please the Father but I know my own weaknesses and my own frailties. I hope there are many like Epaphras who are upholding me in prayer that I will stand firm in all the will of God all the days of my life.

It is our responsibility to pray *'for all the saints'*. We must be careful to do it diligently. This is what 'agonizing' in prayer is all about. It is so easy for us to pray casually for others, if we remember to do so at all. We need to wrestle in prayer for them. We pray until we know we have given it our very best.

This is a great challenge. Prayer in the Spirit is no half-hearted business. It is a serious encounter with God. When we are filled with the Spirit, we are also filled with His concern for our brothers and sisters and His compassion touches us. Love and gentleness and kindness are fruits of the Holy Spirit (Galatians 5:22f.). So these are qualities of praying in the Spirit, too.

We need to remember, however, that we can only pray for others through Jesus. In particular, this means praying on the basis of the cross and the empty tomb. It is only because Christ died for us and rose again that we can approach the Father with confidence and assurance. The writer to the Hebrews puts it well when he says:

> *'Therefore, since we have a great high priest who has gone through the heavens, Jesus the Son of God, let us hold firmly to the faith we profess. For we do not have a high priest who is unable to sympathise with our weaknesses, but we have one who has been tempted in every way, just as we are – yet was without sin. Let us then approach the throne of grace with confidence, so that we may receive mercy and find grace to help us in our time of need ... let us draw near to God with a sincere heart in full assurance of faith, having our hearts sprinkled to cleanse us from a guilty conscience and having our bodies washed with pure water.'*   (Hebrews 4:14–16; 10:22)

It is because Jesus suffered for us and endured the cross and rose again from the tomb that we also can approach God through Him. Jesus is the only true Intercessor. As we pray for one another, we not only do so through Him, but, in a pale way, we reflect His eternal, mediatorial ministry, too.

Prayer is also only possible through the power of the Holy Spirit. He is the enabler, the one who makes it possible for us to pray at all. True prayer is always prayer in the Spirit.

Don't forget

- The throne of grace is one place where we can all meet. No matter who we are or what our differences, when we pray there is only one place we can go. Here is a place of true unity and fellowship.

- When we pray for one another we help one another. When we fail to pray, that help languishes.

- To pray for another person is to use all our energy and effort to struggle on to victory.

- Joining people in their struggle through prayer requires love. It means spending time before God pouring out our hearts in deep and caring concern. It means feeling the pain of those we pray for. It means entering their world, as it were, and somehow participating in their experience.

- To 'agonize' in prayer is to throw everything into it, to pray earnestly and sincerely and passionately, to pray to the best of one's ability. It is not a flash in the pan, some momentary burst of prayer arising from an exciting meeting or an emotional experience of some kind. It is a pattern of life.

- It is so easy for us to pray casually for others, if we remember to do so at all. We need to wrestle in prayer for them. We pray until we know we have given it our very best.

Note

1   W.J. Perschbacher (ed.), *The New Analytical Greek Lexicon* (Peabody, Mass.: Hendrickson, 1990); Liddell and Scott, *A Lexicon (abridged)* (London: Oxford, 1872).

Chapter 7

'He Will Bring Glory to Me...'
(John 16:14)

Prayer in the Spirit is unselfish prayer

Prayer in the Spirit can never be selfish. A moment's reflection makes it obvious that this must be so. Unselfishness is the essence of the Spirit's ministry.

True prayer in the Spirit displays all the qualities of life in the Spirit, for it reflects the character of the Holy Spirit Himself. So self-centred prayers can never be spiritual and spiritual prayers can never be selfish.

The very first New Testament injunction to pray is that we should love our enemies and pray for those who persecute us (Matthew 5:44). James warns us that when we pray to satisfy our own personal ends, our prayers will not be answered.

> *'You want something but don't get it. You kill and covet, but you cannot have what you want. You quarrel and fight. You do not have, because you do not ask God. When you ask, you do not receive, because you ask with wrong motives, that you may spend what you get on your pleasures.'* (James 4:2–3)

We probably don't have to look very far to find examples of the kind of thing James is referring to here. Too often, we don't pray at all. Then when we do pray, we are preoccupied with our own needs. Frequently, these are so pressing we find it hard to think of anything else. Our human bodies shout very loudly most of the time and the sound drowns out all other cries.

When we pray in the Spirit, however, our motives cannot help but be right, for they are initiated by the Spirit Himself. We have strong grounds for affirming this.

To glorify Christ

Firstly, Jesus clearly taught His disciples that the Spirit's major role would be to glorify Him, that He would remind them of His teaching and that He would lead them into truth.

> 'When the Counsellor comes, whom I will send to you from the Father, the Spirit of truth who goes out from the Father, he will testify about me.'   (John 15:26)

> 'But when he, the Spirit of truth, comes, he will guide you into all truth. He will not speak on his own; he will speak only what he hears, and he will tell you what is yet to come. He will bring glory to me by taking from what is mine and making it known to you. All that belongs to the Father is mine. That is why I said the Spirit will take from what is mine and make it known to you.'
> (John 16:13–15)

For the Holy Spirit to assist us in praying for anything that does not bring glory to Jesus is plainly impossible. Hence, it is crucial that we keep in close fellowship with the Holy Spirit so that He can deflect our praying away from our own narrow wishes into the wider and more important affairs of the kingdom of heaven.

When own interests clamour for our attention, it is not easy to hear the softer, gentler cries of the realm of God. So we need the Holy Spirit to awaken our hearts and to sensitize our minds to God's voice.

To paraphrase the words of Jesus, the Spirit of truth will testify about Him. He will guide us into all truth. He will not speak on His own; He will speak only what He hears, and He will tell us what is yet to come. He will bring glory to Christ by taking from what is His and making it known to us (John 15:26; 16:13–15).

It was in 1952 that I first heard about the gifts of the Spirit. I was fascinated and excited about the extraordinary possibilities I now saw opening up before me. But people warned me that those who practised such things were dangerously deluded.

Even worse, they were probably demon-possessed. You only had to attend their meetings to see for yourself – they were noisy, emotional, disorderly and fanatical. People all prayed aloud at the same time. They cried and trembled and spoke in tongues. They got carried away with enthusiasm.

Well, some of that was true. Compared with what I was used to, such gatherings were noisy and emotional. But one thing stood out. This was their love for Christ. I had never encountered people who loved Jesus so much. Their songs were Christ-centred. Their praise was Christ-centred. Their prayers were Christ-centred. Their fellowship was Christ-centred.

If this was the devil, he was clearly very misguided! All he was doing was making people love Jesus more than ever before!

Nothing has happened in the last fifty years to change my opinion about this. Over that time, I have been as aware as anyone of the abuses, heresies and deviations the Pentecostal movement has spawned. As the president of a Bible College, I spend considerable time correcting mistakes in doctrine and endeavouring to impart to my students a balanced, scriptural approach to ministry. Yet for all that, and in spite of the errors, Pentecostalism, and its younger sister, the Charismatic movement, continue to inculcate a fervent love for the Saviour.

Out of this revival have come hundreds of songs of praise. Musicians and songsters all over the world have been inspired by the Holy Spirit to glorify the Lord through melody.

Of course, nowadays, charismatic phenomena are much more widely accepted and the old animosities have largely disappeared. But the point is that when we are immersed in the Spirit and pray in the Spirit, we cannot help but honour the Lord Jesus Christ.

The primacy of Jesus

Jesus taught that the Holy Spirit would not *'speak on his own'* (John 16:13). In other words, He would never act independently of the other members of the Godhead. So everything the Spirit says is consistent with the mind and will of God. Naturally, then, He can only speak those things that honour the Lord.

Secondly, Jesus said the Spirit would bring glory to Him (John 16:14). No matter what the Spirit does, His purpose is to honour the Lord Jesus Christ. When we apply this to prayer, we can see how Spirit-led prayers will always do the same. If we desire to uplift the Lord Jesus in our praying, we need to be Spirit-filled. The more the Spirit is at work in our lives, the more we will fulfil this desire.

Of course, there is much in Scripture about the primacy of Jesus. Here are a few samples:

> *'And God placed all things under his feet and appointed him to be head over everything for the church, which is his body, the fullness of him who fills everything in every way.'*
> (Ephesians 1:22–23)

> *'... at the name of Jesus every knee should bow,*
> *in heaven and on earth and under the earth,*
> *and every tongue confess that Jesus Christ is Lord,*
> *to the glory of God the Father.'* (Philippians 2:10–11)

> *'And he is the head of the body, the church; he is the beginning and the firstborn from among the dead, so that in everything he might have the supremacy.'* (Colossians 1:18)

> *'But grow in the grace and knowledge of our Lord and Saviour Jesus Christ. To him be glory both now and for ever! Amen.'*
> (2 Peter 3:18)

> *'Worthy is the Lamb, who was slain,*
> *to receive power and wealth and wisdom and strength*
> *and honour and glory and praise!'* (Revelation 5:12)

> *'I am the Alpha and the Omega, the First and the Last, the Beginning and the End.'* (Revelation 22:13)

There is no question that honour and glory belong to Jesus Christ. When we pray in the Spirit, we pray in a fashion consistent with this.

Praying through the Scriptures

One way to ensure we focus on Christ is simply to read the Scriptures as we pray. This is an excellent mode of prayer. I often have the Bible open before me while waiting on the Lord. The intermingling of prayer and praise and meditation on the word of God is beautifully enriching.

It is even better to memorize the Word so that whether we have the printed page itself in front of us or not, we can still use it in prayer. To blend our own personal expressions of honour to God with those of the Bible is a fruitful exercise. And as the Holy Spirit is also the author of the Scriptures, when we use the written Word like this, we cannot help but pray in a fashion consistent with the mind of the Spirit.

Of course, it is easy enough to mouth the words, without making them ours. This is why we need the Spirit's fullness to enable us to pray not only in truth but also in Spirit (John 4:24). In this way, the biblical praises of Jesus become internalized and integrated with our own expressions of worship.

As we utter scriptural phrases, the Spirit within us takes them and quickens them, so they come alive and lift our spirits to new heights of worship and exultation of the Lord.

True prayer is prayer in the Spirit. And this prayer always honours Jesus to the full.

Praying for all the saints

So, to go back to where we started, it is obvious that prayers that centre on ourselves or our own needs do not satisfy the criteria of praying in the Spirit.

Paul makes this plain. When he tells us to pray in the Spirit, he specifically urges us to pray for all the saints and for his ministry (Ephesians 6:18). The focus is clearly on others. Additional references to prayer are of the same nature. Paul prays for the Ephesians (1:17ff.; 3:14ff.). Epaphras wrestles in prayer for the Colossians (Colossians 4:12). Timothy is urged to pray for those in authority (1 Timothy 2:1).

This is not to say it is wrong to bring our own needs to God, of course. We are encouraged to ask Him to meet them. Jesus said very plainly:

> *'Until now you have not asked for anything in my name. Ask and you will receive, and your joy will be complete.'*
> (John 16:24)

And again:

> 'Ask and it will be given to you; seek and you will find; knock and the door will be opened to you. For everyone who asks receives; he who seeks finds; and to him who knocks, the door will be opened.'   (Luke 11:9–10)

And again:

> 'You may ask me for anything in my name, and I will do it.'
> (John 14:14)

But no matter what we ask for, the ultimate aim is that the Saviour be glorified. The Holy Spirit cannot assist us to pray any other way!

Don't forget

- Self-centred prayers can never be spiritual and spiritual prayers can never be selfish.

Chapter 8

'In Accordance with God's Will...'
(Romans 8:27)

Prayer in the Spirit is praying according to God's will

Praying in the Spirit is praying according to God's will. Obviously, when we are led by the Holy Spirit in our dialogue with God, we must be praying correctly.

Paul's letter to the Romans tells us as much:

> *'In the same way, the Spirit helps us in our weakness. We do not know what we ought to pray for, but the Spirit himself intercedes for us with groans that words cannot express. And he who searches our hearts knows the mind of the Spirit, because the Spirit intercedes for the saints in accordance with God's will.'*
> (Romans 8:26–27)

One of the great roles of God's Spirit is to help us to pray in the way God wants us to. Often our dilemma is that we don't know what God's purpose is. If we knew, we would gladly pray to that end. But how do you pray when you don't know what is right? Should we beg God to do this or that? Should we plead for one line of action or for another? What is best?

Ascertaining God's will is one of the most serious challenges in the Christian life. I remember as a young Christian agonizing over this issue. How could I know what God wanted for my future? What was His will and purpose for me? Should I take a job or go to university? Should I marry or stay single? Should I be a missionary or a pastor?

I used to spend hours in prayer, trying to understand the purposes of God for me. I can remember being on my knees in my bedroom, almost groaning with a desire to hear from God. How I longed to be certain that I was living in the right way and doing the right things. At that time, I was so earnest, I would even suffer great self-doubt about whether I was walking down the right side of the street or sitting in the correct seat in a train. What if I was in the wrong place and missed sharing the gospel with someone who needed to hear it? What if I was supposed to meet someone or help a person in need and failed because I'd chosen the wrong bus?

As time passed, I learned to trust God more and to rest and relax in Him. Part of this was through understanding both praying and walking in the Spirit.

Of course, sometimes God does not reveal His purpose until He is ready. Habakkuk found this. He longed to understand what God was about, but the only answer he received was,

> *'Look at the nations and watch –*
> *and be utterly amazed.*
> *For I am going to do something in your days*
> *that you would not believe,*
> *even if you were told.'*   (Habakkuk 1:5)

Meanwhile, he was to trust God and leave the matter in His hands (Habakkuk 2:1–4).

The same principle applies to us. We can trust God to assist us in our praying so that we do so in accordance with His will. We may not fully understand all His purpose, but we can still know the peace and assurance that comes from true prayer. For the Spirit of the Lord does know the mind and will of God and He helps us to pray appropriately. Even when we are not aware that the Spirit is leading us, we must accept by faith that He is.

Prayer in the Spirit is consistent with the Word of God

This means firstly that when the Spirit assists us we can never pray anything contrary to the Scriptures. The same Spirit who inspired the written Word of God will inspire our prayers as well. As Matthew Henry aptly says:

> 'The Spirit in the heart never contradicts the Spirit in the word. Those desires that are contrary to the will of God do not come from the Spirit. The Spirit interceding in us evermore melts our wills into the will of God.' [1]

What we have here is a double point of reference. Through prayer in the Spirit, we monitor our Bible reading and continually bathe our study of Scripture with the refreshing streams of prayer. On the other hand, we monitor our praying by ensuring it is contained by the weirs and embankments of Scripture. So the Spirit and the Word work together in a godly balance. The Spirit provides the flow; the Scripture directs it. Jesus laid down this principle clearly when He said,

> '*God is spirit, and his worshippers must worship in spirit and in truth.*'   (John 4:24)

Pray with confidence

Secondly, to pray according to God's will obviously brings with it great confidence. Now we can approach the Lord boldly. John puts it clearly:

> '*This is the confidence we have in approaching God: that if we ask anything according to his will, he hears us. And if we know that he hears us – whatever we ask – we know that we have what we asked of him.*'   (1 John 5:14–15)

What a promise this is! No longer are we beset by uncertainty and hesitancy. When we pray what God wants, we have what God gives. This means that to pray in the Spirit is to pray in faith.

The Lord Jesus Christ had a great deal to say about the power of faith and its ability to transform situations. When His disciples could not heal an epileptic boy, He told them it was because of their unbelief. '*If you have faith as small as a mustard seed,*' He said, '*you can say to this mountain, "Move from here to there" and it will move. Nothing will be impossible for you'* (Matthew 17:20; see also Mark 11:22ff.).

To a centurion, He declared, *'It will be done just as you believed it would'* (Matthew 8:13; Luke 7:9). He asked two blind men, *'Do you believe?'* (Matthew 9:28). He commended a Canaanite woman for her *'great faith'* (Matthew 15:28). He told a synagogue ruler, *'Don't be afraid; just believe'* (Mark 5:36).

When a paralytic's friends brought him to Jesus, He *'saw their faith'* and healed him (Matthew 9:2; Luke 5:20). In His own home town, it was the people's lack of faith which prevented Him from working miracles (Matthew 13:58; Mark 6:6). After cursing a fig tree, Jesus told His disciples they could do similar things by faith (Matthew 21:21–22). When the disciples asked Jesus to increase their faith, He told them that if they believed they could even uproot trees (Luke 17:6)!

This would not be the result of 'praying' but of 'saying'. In other words, Jesus gave them authority to speak to mountains and trees and the like and tell them to move.

When a woman with a haemorrhage was cured, He made the remarkable statement that it was her faith which had healed her (Matthew 9:22; Mark 5:34). He made a similar point to a woman who washed His feet (Luke 7:50). When a grateful leper came to offer Him thanks, He did not tell him that God had healed him but that it was his faith which had made him well (Luke 17:19), and when a blind man was healed, again, it was his faith which healed him (Luke 18:42). Similarly, the apostle Peter declared that it was faith which made a cripple well (Acts 3:16).

In fact, we can almost come to the conclusion that prayer on its own is not enough. Only the prayer of faith is pleasing to God. The point is that faith honours God. When we believe God we are, in effect, declaring that He is trustworthy and powerful. When we don't believe God, we are, in effect, declaring that He cannot be trusted and that His power is limited. To believe God is to compliment Him; to doubt God is to insult Him.

When we fail to trust the Lord and lean on our own understanding and resources we are making a statement that for all our protestations, we really don't trust Him after all.

This is why we must pray in the Spirit. It is the Spirit who helps us to believe God. In fact, unless the Spirit helps us we cannot believe. Even our believing is a gift from God (Ephesians

2:8–9). That is why the disciples asked Jesus to increase their faith (Luke 17:5). They knew they couldn't do it on their own. In the same way, a man whose son was desperately ill asked the Lord, *'Help my unbelief'* (Mark 9:24).

So to pray in the Spirit is to pray in faith. And to pray in faith is to pray in the Spirit.

This shows us how important it is to pray in the Spirit. When we know we have prayed according to God's will, we obviously have confidence that the prayer will be answered. If we are not sure whether what we have prayed is what God wants, then equally obviously we can have little confidence in the result.

'But,' we may ask, 'shouldn't we always pray, "If it be Thy will"?' Surprisingly, the answer is, usually, no. The only biblical precedent for this is what happened with Jesus in Gethsemane. But the circumstances were exceptional. He already knew what God's will for Him was, for He had clearly explained it to His disciples (Matthew 16:21ff.; 17:9; 26:12; John 2:18ff.). In His humanity, He quailed at the prospect of the cross and pleaded with God for an alternative, but finally yielded, saying, *'not as I will, but as you will'* (Matthew 26:39). He clearly knew what God wanted and resolved to submit to it.

Normally, it is our responsibility to discover the will of God from Scripture and through prayer, and then to pray accordingly. If the Lord does not reveal His purposes to us, then we must patiently wait for Him to fulfil His will. The vital thing is to walk in the Spirit so that when we do pray we do so in agreement with the purpose and plan of God.

True prayer requires commitment

It is far more important, then, to live and move and pray in the Spirit than to frame our prayers correctly or to adopt certain times or modes. Even if we don't get the words exactly right, we can still pray according to God's will, as long as we are in the Spirit. This requires dedication and commitment.

It means devoting time to communing with God so the desires of the flesh are crucified and no longer dominate our affections (Galatians 5:24). Often we make the mistake of beginning with our requests rather than our relationship. If we would focus our praying initially on fellowship with God and our need to bring our human desires and longings in line with His will, the rest of our praying would also conform to His will. By walking in the Spirit and not the flesh, we automatically desire those things that God wants.

It means being willing to **linger longer** with the Lord, not dashing in and out of an audience with Him with inappropriate and disrespectful haste (Psalm 84:1–4, 10). In any relationship, extended time is necessary for trust and understanding to develop. Prayer in the Spirit demands relaxed and unhurried communion with God through Christ. Usually, when we begin our prayers, our lives and thinking are so cluttered that even to settle down enough to listen to what the Lord is saying requires time and patience.

We live in an age of instant results, but this does not apply to praying in the Spirit. While God can work very quickly, for our sakes He usually walks with measured tread.

We need to use the Scriptures as we pray and allow God's Word to speak to us and convict us of our sin (Psalm 119:9, 105). This is one of the most common ways in which the Spirit shows us the truths we need to know. Our dulled minds sometimes do not hear the Spirit's voice. But the words of the Bible are clear and plain. We cannot avoid them. They tell us clearly what is sin and what is not. We ignore this at our peril.

It means being filled with the Spirit all the time (Ephesians 5:18). When we are in the Spirit and God's Spirit is in us, we pray according to His will and so we confidently expect an answer. This is true praying in the Spirit.

Don't forget

- The Spirit provides the flow of prayer; the Scripture directs it.
- When we pray what God wants, we have what God gives.
- Often we make the mistake of beginning with our requests rather than our relationship.
- To pray in the Spirit is to pray in faith.
- We need to **linger longer** with the Lord.

Note

1   Matthew Henry, *Matthew Henry's Commentary*, Vol. VI (New York: Fleming H. Revell, n.d.), p. 422.

Chapter 9

'The Fruit of the Spirit Is Love...'
(Galatians 5:22)

Praying in the Spirit means walking in the Spirit

In his letter to the Galatians, Paul clearly contrasts the fruit of
the Holy Spirit with the works of the flesh. The two, he points
out, are plainly opposite to each other. If we walk in the flesh,
we are not in the Spirit; if we walk in the Spirit, we are not in the
flesh. The same may be said of our praying:

> 'So I say, walk in the Spirit, and you will not gratify the
> desires of the flesh. For the flesh desires what is contrary to
> the Spirit, and the Spirit what is contrary to the flesh. They
> are in conflict with each other, so that you do not do what
> you want.' (Galatians 5:16–18 NIV, modified)

The language could not be plainer. If we walk in the flesh, our
lives are out of tune with the Spirit. If we pray in the flesh,
our prayers are out of tune with the Spirit. It is impossible to
pray in the Spirit without walking in the Spirit. But if we do walk
in the Spirit, then our praying will be consistent with the life of
the Spirit.

When we walk in the Spirit, our lives are characterized by
love, joy, peace, patience, kindness, goodness, faithfulness,
gentleness and self-control (Galatians 5:22–23). This is not to
say that we will never be unloving or sad or unfaithful. But it is
to affirm that, by and large, these qualities stand out. Just as a
tree is known by its fruit, so are we. There may occasionally be

individual pieces of bad fruit, but, overall, our lives are identifiable by the sweet fruit we bear.

We tend to think it is presumptuous to expect our lives to be characterized by such qualities. Surely we are sinners who can never do any better than muddle our way through? The truth is that when we think like this we are really insulting God! He gives us His Holy Spirit so we **can** bear good fruit. Our lives **should** be characterized by such qualities. The fruit of the Spirit is never out of season. When Jesus said, *'By their fruit you will recognise them'* (Matthew 7:20), He meant it. Bad trees are known by their fruit – and so are good ones. If we are not daily demonstrating the fruit of the Spirit, something is seriously wrong with our lives.

Now, not one of these qualities panders to our own cravings: they all respond to the needs and desires of others. Hence, they form a clear contrast to the works of the flesh which are all self-centred. So as our lives are characterized by this gracious fruit, our prayers automatically focus on unselfish interests.

It is a contradiction in terms to claim to walk in the Spirit if we do not pray in the Spirit. When we pray in the Spirit, we offer prayers of love and kindness and gentleness and faithfulness. Such praying is not identified by the degree of fervour or noise or emotion or eloquence displayed – it is recognized by its nature. True prayer in the Spirit is generous and unselfish. It's as simple as that.

Paul puts it very plainly when he tells us that if we walk in the Spirit we will not satisfy the desires of the flesh (Galatians 5:16). This is not a command, it is a promise. If we walk in the Spirit, it is impossible to obey the demands of the flesh. The same may be said of prayer. When we pray in the Spirit, we cannot pray in the flesh.

Love

When we pray in the Spirit, our requests are motivated by love. This means we pray with the best interests of others at heart. The nature of love means things cannot be otherwise. How can we pray selfish or self-centred prayers when our hearts are filled with love? It is interesting that in exhorting the Ephesians to pray in the Spirit, Paul talks only of praying for others (Ephesians 6:18, 19).

Joy

Prayer in the Spirit is also full of joy (Galatians 5:22). The joy of the Lord becomes our strength as we draw near to Him. We rejoice with indescribable joy and we celebrate His love and salvation. No matter how serious a matter we may be presenting to God, there will always be an undercurrent of effervescent joy. It cannot be contained. The spring of joy will flow even if a mountain of sadness lies above it. It will find a way out somewhere. With joy we draw water from the wells of salvation (Isaiah 12:3).

Peace

There is a deep, settled peace when we pray in the Spirit (Galatians 5:22). We do not always know how the Lord is responding to our prayers or how He will deal with them. But we know He will respond and we know He will deal with them wisely and well. Many times, I have brought a concern to God and almost instantly, before I have had time even to vocalize the need, I have experienced a deep sense of peace, a conviction that all is well and everything will turn out all right. God's peace is usually instantaneous and spontaneous. It is the reassurance of the Spirit that our prayers are on track.

Patience

When we pray truly, God's Spirit gives us patience (Galatians 5:22). How often have we prayed but the answer has not come when we expected it! We usually want things wrapped up by the next morning. God is normally not in such a hurry. Often He invites us to wait until the time is right. When we pray in the Spirit, His patience enables us to trust quietly in Him and to wait for the day of His power. Isaiah puts it succinctly when he writes:

> 'So this is what the Sovereign LORD says:
> "See, I lay a stone in Zion,
>   a tested stone,
> a precious cornerstone for a sure foundation;
>   the one who trusts will never be dismayed."'   (Isaiah 28:16)

Christ is the sure foundation. He will not be moved. So we can rest securely on Him, without dismay. It is interesting that the latter part of this verse literally reads, 'the one who trusts in him will not be in haste.' In other words, when we pray to the Lord, the pressure is off. There is no need to panic. We know that everything is under control. So we are patient, knowing He will respond in His own good time.

Kindness

Kindness is another feature of praying in the Spirit (Galatians 5:22). No matter what others have done to us or how they feel about us, we will pray about them in a kindly way. The Greek word for 'kind' is *chrestos*. It is a word used by Jesus to describe good wine – wine that is mellow, warming and healing (Luke 5:39). Kind praying is like this. It cries to God for Him to do good to others, to bless them, to reassure them, to comfort them.

Goodness

When we pray in the Spirit, our prayers are 'good' (Galatians 5:22). There is nothing corrupt or evil or bad about them. Naturally, this must be so. The Spirit is good and so must our prayers be. It is impossible, then, to pray for anything vindictive or vengeful. We cannot call down curses or ask God to do anything immoral. Spirit-infused prayers are by nature good.

Faithfulness

God is faithful. Time and again, the Scripture affirms this. The psalmist vows to make God's faithfulness known to all generations (Psalm 89:1). Jeremiah declares, *'great is your faithfulness'* (Lamentations 3:23). Paul says over and over, *'God is faithful'* (1 Corinthians 10:13; 1 Thessalonians 5:24; 2 Thessalonians 3:3).

Obviously, when we pray in the Spirit, we pray faithfully (Galatians 5:22). The Spirit, who is faithful, also enables us to be faithful in our calling upon God. Just as He is dependable, so now are we. Like Samuel, we can say, *'As for me, far be it from me that I should sin against the LORD by failing to pray for you'* (1 Samuel 12:23). Faithfully, we continue to pray.

Gentleness

Spiritual prayers are gentle prayers. They are neither aggressive nor angry. As gentleness is a fruit of the Spirit (Galatians 5:23), so it is a quality of prayer. Some people shout at God as if He has to be persuaded or convinced or badgered into hearing us. Like the prophets of Baal, they go to frantic extremes to gain a hearing (1 Kings 18:28). Not that there is anything wrong in itself with shouting. There is plenty of biblical precedent for it (e.g. Psalm 95; Acts 4:24). But it must be for the right reason. Obviously, it is fitting and proper to raise our voices for joy or delight or in a shout of victory. In fact, Jesus said that if we do not do so, the very stones might cry out (Luke 19:40)! But raising our voices will do nothing in itself to influence God. When we pray in the Spirit, we know God hears us, whether we shout or not. Even the unspoken, yearning whisper of the heart is known to Him. Gentleness is a mark of true prayer.

Humility

It is worth noting that the Greek word for 'gentleness' can also mean 'humility'. So when we pray in the Spirit, we also pray humbly. We come to God in the name of Jesus and trusting in His merits alone. There is no work of righteousness for which we can claim merit. We cannot rely on the length or intensity of our prayers to impress God. Prayers are not answered as rewards for our hard work. It is in humility that we approach God, knowing that by the Spirit we will be heard.

Self-control

Finally, self-control is a quality of spiritual praying (Galatians 5:23). As we have noted already, there is no prescribed form of prayer. We can pray silently or aloud. We can shout and dance and sing or lie in holy awe on our faces. We can experience powerful emotions or we can be quietly impassive. Any or all of these may be right at different times. We can utter thoughtfully prepared orisons or spontaneous outpourings in tongues. But whatever form we use, it will never be out of control. Self-control is a fruit of the Spirit. Wild, unrestrained behaviour is never appropriate in true prayer. When people lose control of their emotions or their behaviour is unseemly or offensive, the Spirit is not there. Praying in the Spirit is marked by self-control.

It is also evidenced by discipline. This means an organized, regular prayer life, with programmed times set aside for this purpose. Some people seem to believe that prayer in the Spirit can only be spontaneous and that if we organize it, we kill it. To them, a regular pattern of prayer is inconceivable. They see it as legalistic and lifeless. To them prayer is extemporaneous, unrehearsed and impromptu. To pray at a given time because it is time to pray, whether you feel like it or not, is unthinkable. Prayer should be the overflowing of the heart. Otherwise it is not sincere.

Of course, there is some truth in this. Prayer should take place all the time, day and night, as we continually delight in our fellowship with Father. But this does not obviate the need for structured and concentrated times of prayer. As the fruit of the Spirit includes self-mastery, so does prayer in the Spirit. We cannot survive on casual conversations with God. We need times of uninterrupted communion with Him.

I am grateful to my Baptist mentors who, when I first became a Christian, taught me the inestimable value of a daily 'quiet time', in which to pray and read the Word without distraction. Today, over fifty years later, I still observe this practice. I think I can safely say that this has been one of the greatest single factors in my spiritual growth. Regular, disciplined, sustained prayer is crucial to true spirituality.

Crucified with Christ

It is significant that at this point Paul reminds us that we have been crucified with Christ. It is through identification with Him in this way that the flesh *'with its passions and desires'* is put to death (Galatians 5:24). The cross is always central to every true Christian activity for it continually brings us face to face with the issue of self and our need to deny our own desires for Jesus' sake. So every day

> *'We always carry around in our body the death of Jesus, so that the life of Jesus may also be revealed in our body.'*
>
> (2 Corinthians 4:10)

Herman Ridderbos puts it well when he writes:

> '[Believers] share His cross ... So the lordship of the flesh
> and its passions is also denied. This is part of what was
> overcome on the cross. Hence it can be said of those who
> are of Christ that they have crucified the flesh. There came
> a moment of time in their lives in which they were taken
> up into that fellowship of life, and in which, therefore, the
> dominion of the flesh over them was broken.'[1]

When Jesus was being crucified He prayed for forgiveness for
those who crucified Him. *'Father, forgive them,'* He said, *'for they
do not know what they are doing'* (Luke 23:34). In the midst of the
most extenuating circumstances, when every nerve and fibre of
His body was screaming in agony and every single one of His
senses was crying out for attention, sympathy and relief from
the exquisite agony of His suffering, He was still able to think
of the even greater distress and far more dreadful condition of
those who were killing Him. Their need for forgiveness from sin
gripped His attention more than His own need of release from
pain.

This is praying in the Spirit. It is praying according to
God's will rather than our own. It is seeing things from God's
perspective. It is being more moved by the passion of the Spirit
than the lust of the flesh. It is being impelled to action by the
heart of God, not the heart of man.

Normally, when we pray, it is a good idea to find a time and
place where we are removed from the distractions of everyday
life, so we can concentrate on the things of God. A once-
popular hymn put it like this:

> 'I come to the garden alone,
> While the dew is still on the roses,
> And the voice I hear
> Falling on my ear
> The Son of God discloses.
> And he walks with me,
> And he talks with me,
> And he tells me I am his own;
> And the joy we share as we tarry there
> None other has ever known.'   (C. Austin Miles)

If you wanted to find a place like this to pray – where there are few distractions; where there is an atmosphere of tranquillity and peace; where you can relax and focus your attention on the closeness of the Spirit; where bodily desires and fleshly demands can be put aside; where the sweet presence of God surrounds you like the cool, balmy breezes of a bright spring morning; where the joy of the Lord rises up within you like the marvellous welling up of first love – if you wanted to find such a place, you would not choose a Roman cross! But it was on a cross that Jesus showed more than anywhere else the power of godly prayer. For here, where there were none of those advantages, where torturing pain was arching every muscle and wild distractions were howling around Him like demons, He was still able to focus on the will and purpose of the Father and to pray a godly prayer.

Walking in the Spirit is walking under the shadow of Calvary. So praying in the Spirit is praying in the spirit of the cross. It means praying unselfishly, with the same attitude Jesus displayed in His living, praying and dying for us.

Don't forget

- It is impossible to pray in the Spirit without walking in the Spirit.
- The fruit of the Spirit is never out of season.
- True prayer in the Spirit is generous and unselfish. It's as simple as that.
- When we pray in the Spirit, we know God hears us, whether we shout or not. Even the unspoken, yearning whisper of the heart is known to Him. Gentleness is a mark of true prayer.
- We cannot survive on casual conversations with God. We need times of uninterrupted communion with Him.
- Walking in the Spirit is walking under the shadow of Calvary. So praying in the Spirit is praying in the spirit of the cross.

Note

1   H. Ridderbos, 'The Epistle of Paul to the Churches of Galatia' in *The New International Commentary on the New Testament* (Grand Rapids: Eerdmans, 1972), p. 209.

Chapter 10

'Keep Your Spiritual Fervour'
(Romans 12:11)

Praying in the Spirit means praying fervently

Praying in the Spirit means praying fervently.

Many people are afraid of becoming too emotional. There have been so many warnings against going overboard in this area, that it is easy to be wary of it. But if our praying is to be infused with the Spirit of God, how can it be other than deeply emotional? Like the two disciples on the road to Emmaus, when we talk with the Lord, our hearts 'burn within us' (Luke 24:32).

What else can we expect as we draw near to God and realize again the wonder of His love and the miracle of grace? If this does not excite us, what hope do we have?

The world has duped us in this regard. It has been so critical of emotion in religion that we have become embarrassed about it. We don't want to be labelled as fanatical or extremist. Yet the same people who look down their noses at emotion in religion, will shout, jump, cheer, weep, embrace, laugh and bite their nails at an athlete winning a race or hitting a ball or kicking a goal and think nothing of it!

On 26 January 1993, the West Indies defeated Australia by one run in a long Test Cricket match. Towards the end, in an apparently hopeless position, the last two Australian batsmen stubbornly defended their wickets and, one by one, painstakingly added runs to the score. It dawned on the home crowd that victory might still be possible. They clapped every run made as if it were six! The suspense in the air was tangible, even over the radio. Yet when there is a similar emotion-charged atmosphere in a Christian meeting, we are warned that things are getting out of hand.

When Andre Agassi won Wimbledon and dropped to his knees on the court, the crowd cheered. Had he shown such emotion in church, he might have been dismissed as an extremist.

Ironically enough, the word 'fan', which is universally acceptable, is actually an abbreviation of 'fanatic', which many people find distasteful! Most of the time, it is pride that prevents us from becoming emotional about God. We are worried about what people might think. When we are alone in prayer, however, this can hardly be an issue. God's Spirit can touch our hearts and gently move us till we are soft before Him. If we weep, who is there to know or care? If we laugh, what will it matter?

I am not for one moment advocating uncontrolled emotion. We have already seen how self-control is a mark of the Spirit's presence. Lack of control is never appropriate. But over-control is also problematic. If our hearts are too restricted to respond to God, we are, to quote Paul in another context, of all people 'most miserable'.

Prayer in the Spirit arouses emotion

Human beings are emotional. Much of the time we are more driven by emotion than by reason. We tend to act intuitively rather than rationally. Every complete human experience embraces the intellect, the emotions and the volition. Or putting it more simply, knowing, feeling and willing. This includes Christian experience. There is an intellectual aspect – we hear and understand the gospel. There is an emotional response – we sense our own need and the drawing power of the love of God. There is a volitional action – we decide, as an act of will, to follow Jesus. These three elements should always be present in our walk with the Lord.

The renowned English poet William Wordsworth wrote,

'Poetry is the spontaneous overflow of powerful feelings: it takes its origin from emotion recollected in tranquility.'[1]

There are similarities between worship and poetry. Prayer might also be described as 'the spontaneous overflow of powerful feelings' which finds its source in contemplation of God.

In a similar vein, the nineteenth-century scholar Matthew Arnold wrote,

> 'The true meaning of religion is thus not simply morality, but morality touched by emotion.'[2]

Prayer on fire with the Spirit

In Scripture, fire is frequently associated with the Holy Spirit. This is no accident. John the Baptist proclaimed that Jesus would baptize with the Holy Spirit and fire (Matthew 3:11f.). At Pentecost, something like flames of fire were seen (Acts 2:1–4). Paul encourages the Thessalonians not to put out the Spirit's fire (1 Thessalonians 5:19). The major focus here is on holiness. The fire of the Spirit is to purify and sanctify us. Just as chaff is destroyed by fire after the harvest, so the Holy Spirit destroys those aspects of our living that are of no use to God (Matthew 3:11f.; Luke 3:16f.; cf. 1 Peter 1:2).

But there are also echoes of a deep, burning experience of God as well. So Paul writes,

> *'Never be lacking in zeal, but keep your spiritual fervour.'*
> (Romans 12:11)

We could translate the first part of this statement as 'Don't be lazy or idle in regard to zeal'. The image is of someone lying around listlessly, unwilling to make any effort. The second part of the statement reads literally, 'Boil with the spirit'.

Whether it is the human spirit or the Holy Spirit intended here, is not clear. Paul could be urging us to keep our own spirits on the boil, as it were. Or, he could be saying, 'Keep yourself bubbling with the help of the Holy Spirit'. Either way, in practical terms, the end result is the same. An identical expression is used to describe Apollos, one of the great New Testament teachers. When he spoke, he was 'boiling in spirit' (Acts 18:25). The New Revised Standard Version depicts him graphically as speaking with 'burning enthusiasm'. Such fervour must be a feature of prayer in the Spirit as well. When we pray, we pray fervently, enthusiastically, emotionally.

The Religious Affections is a classic study of Christian experience. It was written in 1746 by the great eighteenth-century philosopher and revivalist Jonathan Edwards. In it he says, 'He who has no religious affection is in a state of spiritual death' and that it is one of the ploys of Satan to 'bring all religion to a mere lifeless formality'.[3] He goes even further and says that 'the things of religion take hold of men's souls no further than they affect them.' He argues that, in his experience, he had never seen anyone converted without their affections being involved.

Edwards goes to some pains to point out that affections arise from the will and the inclination of the heart, rather than physical feelings, yet he also makes it clear that bodily sensations are irrevocably involved. In fact, 'never is there any case whatsoever' where the affections are aroused without the body being affected. Furthermore, Edwards frequently specifically names such qualities as hope, fear, love, hatred, desire, joy, sorrow, compassion and zeal as affections – all of which could be equally well designated emotions. 'Upon the whole,' he concludes, 'I think it clearly and abundantly evident that true religion lies very much in the affections'.[4]

Emotions must be tested

Edwards wisely shows that emotional experiences must be carefully tested. Firstly, they must be consistent with Scripture. If they are not, no matter how powerful they are, they must be rejected (cf. Deuteronomy 13:1–3). Secondly, they must be confirmed by a genuine lifestyle. If our lives do not show evidence of the fruit of the Spirit, our experiences are valueless (Galatians 5:16ff.).

On the other hand, however, if we really do love God and we have a genuine belief in the power of the cross, how can we not be moved by the gospel? Edwards considers the sterile and unmoving attitude of some congregations, and asks in wonder:

'How can they sit and hear of the infinite height, and depth, and length, and breadth of the love of God in Christ

Jesus, of His giving His infinitely dear Son, to be offered up a sacrifice for the sins of men, and of the unparalleled love of the innocent, and holy, and tender Lamb of God, manifested in His dying agonies, His bloody sweat, His loud and bitter cries, and bleeding heart ... and yet be cold and heavy, insensible and regardless?' [5]

Emotion and religious experience played a significant role in the great evangelical awakenings of the eighteenth century. It is only in recent years that evangelicalism has reacted against experience as a validation of the truth.

Again, as Edwards found, part of the problem may be the difficulty of definition. If by 'experience' we only mean 'emotion' we clearly are treading on dangerous ground. However, if by 'experience' we mean a tangible, experiential encounter with the living God, what possible objection could there be?

Pray with passion

There are times when we need to cry out to God with deep feeling. Our passion may be so earnest that, as Eli did with Hannah, when she yearned for a baby son and poured her heart out to God, an outside observer might even think we are drunk (1 Samuel 1:10–18)!

There are other times when, like Jacob, we encounter the Lord with such desperation that we refuse to give up. Jacob struggled with an angel all night, but even then, when the messenger of God tried to leave, Jacob cried, *'I will not let you go unless you bless me'* (Genesis 32:26). This is the earnest prayer of a passionate man. There is nothing casual about it. It is laying hold of God in a way that is content with nothing less than His blessing.

Ludwig von Zinzendorf, the founder of the Moravian Church, whose focus on prayer and mission has already been mentioned, said, 'I have one passion – it is He.'

Some years ago, a young African named Paul Roshi attended Bible College in Australia. When he came among us, he taught us how to pray, not by giving lectures on the subject, but by doing it. For long periods of time, he would pour out his soul to God in earnest prayer, often with tears. He would pray for the

College, for Australia, for Africa, for the world! Today, he is again in Africa, serving God as an evangelist.

When John Alexander Dowie (1875–1907), whose ministry of divine healing around the world is legendary, was ministering in Sydney, Australia, in 1876, he wrote to his fiancée in Adelaide:

> 'To get spirit and temper, we need much prayer, and retiring from the bustle, need to seek God in the stillness ... I say to you, Jeannie dear, get often alone with God ...
>
> I am very frail and very faithless, often it seems to me, but the[se] words breathe my desires and hopes and strivings to be what Christ would have me be.'[6]

We need to rediscover both the passion of prayer and the prayer of passion!

The Lord Jesus Christ had a stern warning for the church at Laodicea:

> *'To the angel of the church in Laodicea write: These are the words of the Amen, the faithful and true witness, the ruler of God's creation. I know your deeds, that you are neither cold nor hot. I wish you were either one or the other! So, because you are lukewarm – neither hot nor cold – I am about to spit you out of my mouth.'*   (Revelation 3:14–16)

What solemn words! Sadly, they reflect very much the spiritual state of much of our praying today. If the Lord were to address the contemporary Church, would He find it necessary to say the same things? So often, our praying is insipid and tepid. It is not that we don't pray at all; we do. But our prayers lack fire! They do not move our own hearts, let alone the heart of God.

Rekindle the flame

It is time to do as Paul exhorted Timothy – to stir up the embers of the charisma of the Spirit within us and stoke the fire again.

> *'For this reason I remind you to fan into flame the gift of God, which is in you through the laying on of my hands.'*
>
> (2 Timothy 1:6)

This principle applies to prayer. The flames of affection need to be stoked regularly, lest they die away and the coals of love grow cold. When our hearts are no longer moved by the love of Christ we are in deep trouble.

It is the Holy Spirit's role to bring Christ to us. The more we are filled with the Spirit, the more we enable Him to fulfil this purpose – and the more the glory and wonder of Christ moves our affections and stirs our spirits.

Inasmuch as life in the Spirit is firmly based on Scripture, it satisfies the enquiry of the mind. Inasmuch as it is also experienced in the emotions, it fulfils the yearnings of the heart.

To pray in the Spirit is to pray with both faith and fervour.

Don't forget

- Praying in the Spirit means praying fervently.

- God's Spirit can touch our hearts and gently move us till we are soft before Him. If we weep, who is there to know or care? If we laugh, what will it matter?

- Fervour is a feature of prayer in the Spirit. When we pray, we pray fervently, enthusiastically, emotionally.

- The earnest prayer of a passionate human being has nothing casual about it. It is laying hold of God in a way that is content with nothing less than His blessing.

- We need to rediscover both the passion of prayer and the prayer of passion!

Notes

1   William Wordsworth, *Lyrical Ballads*, 1798.
2   Matthew Arnold, *Literature and Dogma*, 1873.
3   Jonathan Edwards (Edinburgh: The Banner of Truth Trust, [1746] 1984), p. 49.
4   ibid., pp. 24–31, 47.
5   ibid., p. 52.
6   E. Sheldrake (ed.), *The Personal Letters of John Alexander Dowie* (Zion City: W.G. Voliva, 1912), pp. 91, 92.

Chapter 11

'That They May Be One...'
(John 17:21)

Prayer in the Spirit produces unity

Prayer in the Spirit produces unity. It brings people together. There is one Spirit and there is one body. Prayers that enhance this are true prayers. Those that breed division are not. By definition, they cannot be.

Jesus made this startlingly clear in His great high priestly prayer (John 17). There can be no doubt that when Jesus prayed He did so in the Spirit. The Spirit was given to Him without measure and His whole life was anointed by the Spirit (John 3:34; Luke 4:18; Acts 10:38). So when He communed with God, the Spirit was there. And unity was a major focus of His petition:

> *'My prayer is not for them alone. I pray also for those who will believe in me through their message, that all of them may be one, Father, just as you are in me and I am in you. May they also be in us so that the world may believe that you have sent me. I have given them the glory that you gave me, that they may be one as we are one: I in them and you in me. May they be brought to complete unity to let the world know that you sent me and have loved them even as you have loved me.'*   (John 17:20–23)

Note the regular occurrence here of phrases like *'may be one'* and *'complete unity'*. Jesus intended us all to be together in faith and love and He prayed to this end.

Unity of the Spirit

Similarly, when we pray truly, unity will be a major focus. Paul stresses this in His letter to the Ephesians:

> 'As a prisoner for the Lord, then, I urge you to live a life worthy of the calling you have received. Be completely humble and gentle; be patient, bearing with one another in love. Make every effort to keep the unity of the Spirit through the bond of peace. There is one body and one Spirit – just as you were called to one hope when you were called – one Lord, one faith, one baptism; one God and Father of all, who is over all and through all and in all.'
> (Ephesians 4:1–6)

Again, note the emphasis here on unity. The word 'one' occurs seven times. There is one body, one Spirit, one hope, one Lord, one faith, one baptism, one God and Father of all. The unity of the Spirit on earth is a clear reflection of the unity that already exists in heaven. It is important to note that this is not something we have to create, but rather a condition we are to maintain. '*Keep the unity of the Spirit,*' urges Paul.

Praying for one another is a sure way to obey this injunction. It is hard to be angry with people when we pray for them! How can we fight with someone we have lifted up before God in caring concern? How many of our divisions would disappear if we prayed for each other with deeper earnestness and more genuine affection?

The old spiritual puts it wisely:

> 'You can talk about me as much as you please,
> I'll talk about you down on my knees!'

If we did this more often, we would work together much better and display the love of Jesus more effectively to the world. Jesus taught that it would be through our love for each other that we proved to be His disciples (John 13:35). How miserably we have failed in this! Yet by praying in the Spirit, we can begin to achieve it. Lifting each other up before the Lord is at least a start.

It was an outpouring of the Spirit at Herrnhut in Moravia in 1727 that initiated the prayer watch which lasted day and night continuously for the next ten decades. For three years there had been factionalism and dissension. When the Spirit came, the conflict left! The resultant unity made possible the greatest prayer vigil in Christian history – one hundred years of un-interrupted waiting on God!

Through the influence of these Moravians, John and Charles Wesley were converted. The result was the great Wesleyan revival that changed the course of history and touched the whole world. It is interesting to reflect on the potential that lies with us today as we pray together and work together as one.

One encouraging feature of the closing decade of the twenti-eth century was a resurgence of prayer. All over the world, there were prayer conferences, prayer rallies, prayer seminars, prayer vigils and prayer gatherings. Thousands of people met together to pray for their communities and to cry out to God for a visitation from on high. Often they came from different churches and denominations, uniting together in common purpose before the throne of God. In Australia, in 2001, a chain of prayer was initiated for twenty-four hours every day in which hundreds of churches and thousands of people participated, possibly the greatest sustained time of prayer in the nation's history. There is no doubt God's favour rests on His people when they wait before Him like this. The psalmist puts it well:

> *'How good and how pleasant it is*
> *when brothers live together in unity!...*
> *For there the LORD bestows his blessing,*
> *even life for evermore.'*   (Psalm 133:1, 3)

Unity of prayer

Unity of doctrine has been a stumbling block for Christians since the first century. There are always areas of disagreement. This is partly the result of our own perverseness. We simply will not listen to each other or try to understand one another's view. On the other hand, there are many areas where there is room for different understandings of the Scriptures. It is not necessary for us to agree about everything.

Perhaps we have made a mistake in attempting to build unity on theological or biblical agreement. A better place to start could be in prayer. At least we can pray for each other. This is clearly possible, even with people whose doctrines may be far removed from ours. The Lord told us to pray for our enemies (Luke 6:27f.). So we can certainly pray for our friends! When we do this, the result will be an increasing desire to have fellowship with those for whom we pray. Whether we share the same convictions about doctrine or not, we can pray together. This is where the unity of the Spirit begins.

A man once challenged me about attending a conference where there were Catholics present. 'How can you worship alongside a Catholic?' he demanded. 'You should walk out of the meeting!'

'So what am I to do?' I responded. 'Catholics are not the only ones with whom I might disagree. Do you want me to interrogate every person in the building before the service to make sure we have a theological basis for unity?'

Again, let me explain that I am very much concerned about theology. My life is given to teaching and studying Scripture. I demand of my students that they always supply biblical evidence for the things they believe. But if we are to wait until we all agree on doctrine before we work together, we will be waiting a very long time! Meanwhile, we can join in prayer. This is one area where the one Spirit of God can remind us that we are one body and assist us to maintain unity.

One of the great by-products of the Charismatic renewal has been the co-operation it has produced. David du Plessis, known in his lifetime as 'Mr Pentecost' because of his ministry of introducing the baptism and gifts of the Spirit to people of all churches, used to say that true renewal was both charismatic and ecumenical. That is, it was identifiable by the expression of both spiritual gifts and unity.

This was certainly true of the late twentieth-century renewal. In its early days, in the 1960s and 1970s in particular, people of all churches got together freely to celebrate their new liberty of love and fellowship. There were great national and international conferences in which Catholics and Protestants rejoiced together, literally joining hands in worship and celebration. William MacDonald argues that glossolalia 'has a way of uniting Christians who have been theologically deadlocked for centuries.' He goes on to say:

'Among the gifts it appears that no gift has been so instrumental as glossolalia in bringing together spiritually responsive peoples of diverse and conflicting denominational traditions. When in the past four and a half centuries since the Reformation have so many denominational believers witnessed such a degree of unity as in charismatic prayer-and-share meetings? The union that ecclesiologists have not been able to engineer seems to be of no real consequence to the charismatics ... they are discovering the deep sense of unity already existing in the will and spirit of Christ.' [1]

In subsequent years, there was an attempt to draw back behind denominational barriers, in the hope of renewing the denominations. While this has much to commend it, it resulted in a loss of momentum in many cases, and a dying down of the fire. I wonder if, in fact, it displeased the Lord? The Spirit was poured out, among other things, to open us again to unity and fellowship with one another. Did we turn our backs both on each other and the Holy Spirit by our actions?

Certainly, God's Spirit breaks down barriers and helps us to love each other in a refreshing way. When we are truly Spirit-filled, the old inhibitions which make us stand-offish and remote seem to be cast aside. We delight in each other and appreciate each other, whatever our tradition.

No compromise

Over many years, it has been my privilege to preach in churches of all denominations. Week by week my wife and I find ourselves switching rapidly from traditional liturgical worship to free-flowing Pentecostal praise, to almost everything in between. Sometimes, I am asked not to say or do certain things in case they upset someone. At one church, they were cautious about having me speak in the actual service, as I was not ordained in their denomination. So they followed the order of service right through to the benediction and then asked me to preach afterwards!

I never have to compromise anything. But I have learned to adapt. And almost everywhere Vanessa and I go, we find a harmony of prayer and faith, even where there might be serious doctrinal issues, if we chose to focus on them. To be honest, sometimes, even in prayer, things are expressed to which we cannot say 'Amen'. This is a genuine difficulty. In those cases, we just hold our peace and choose not to respond. But where we can, we do. And by and large, we find that prayer is one of the greatest means of rapport.

To pray in the Spirit means to pray in unity with our brothers and sisters in the faith. Because of the prejudices and barriers we have tended to erect over the years, we need the Spirit's help to break through. We cannot do it truly without Him. How desperately we need to be filled with God's Spirit and to walk in the Spirit! Every day, we are dependent on the Holy Spirit to enable us to pray as we ought. It is interesting that the major reason for Paul's suggesting that the Corinthians were not spiritual, was their disunity (1 Corinthians 3:1–4).

Jesus prayed that we might all be one as He and the Father are one (John 17:20–23). Naturally, we cannot be one in the divine sense of the unity of the Godhead. But we can be united in love as are the Father and the Son. And this is the work of the Holy Spirit. He brings us into oneness. This is the basis of praying in the Spirit. It is also the result.

Don't forget

- Prayers that enhance unity are true prayers. Those that breed division are not.
- It is hard to be angry with people when we pray for them.
- We have made a mistake in attempting to build unity on theological or biblical agreement. A better place to start could be in prayer.
- The Lord told us to pray for our enemies (Luke 6:27f.). So we can certainly pray for our friends!
- Whether we share the same convictions about doctrine or not, we can pray together. This is where the unity of the Spirit begins.

- To pray in the Spirit means to pray in unity with our brothers and sisters in the faith.

Note

1   W. MacDonald (1973) in W.E. Mills (ed.), *Speaking in Tongues: a Guide to Research in Glossolalia* (Grand Rapids: Eerdmans, 1986), p. 229.

Chapter 12

'Sighs Too Deep for Words'
(Romans 8:26)[1]

The Holy Spirit helps us to pray

Strangely enough, although what we need to do most is to pray, this is the very thing that in ourselves we cannot do! We depend utterly on the Holy Spirit to help us (Romans 8:26–27). Unless He comes to our aid, our prayers are futile. So prayer in the Spirit is an expression of our human weakness.

Frank Macchia puts it succinctly:

> 'As Heschel stated, "in no other act [but prayer] does humanity experience so often the disparity between the desire for expression and the means of expression." The closer one draws to the divine mystery, the more urgent it becomes to express oneself and, concomitantly, the less able one is to find adequate expression.'[2]

This is our great dilemma. The more we realize our need to pray, the more we are confronted with our inability to do so. How much we need the Spirit's help in this! We have two problems. We are both weak and ignorant. Firstly, we lack the strength to pray effectively. In our humanity, we cannot do anything properly. All we do is marred and limited by the infirmities of the flesh. Secondly, we don't know what to pray for anyway. We are aware of our needs, of course, but what should we ask for? What is the best answer? We do not know. Thankfully, the Holy Spirit comes to our aid.

Inexpressible groans

The strongest statement about praying in the Spirit occurs in
Paul's letter to the Romans. In a nutshell, the apostle shows
how in this way the Holy Spirit helps us to express the
inexpressible. What we cannot put into words, the Holy Spirit
enables us to communicate *'with groans that words cannot
express'* (Romans 8:26). It is interesting to consider what Paul
meant by this.

The word 'groans' is used elsewhere to describe the cries of
sorrow of the Israelites when they were slaves in Egypt (Acts
7:34). It is also used in verse 23 of Romans 8 to describe our
longing for heaven. *'In the same way,'* says Paul, *'the Spirit
helps us.'*

In other words, just as the Hebrews longed for deliverance
from Egypt, and just as we yearn and pine for heaven, so the
Holy Spirit intercedes for us in a personal way which *'words
cannot express'*. When we feel entrapped by the vicissitudes of
life; when there is a dark cloud of heaviness upon us; when we
are hemmed in and there is nowhere to turn; when our broken
hearts cry out to God in anguish for some relief, some easing of
the load; when our spirits feel limp and listless, and our energies
seem drained; when we turn with longing eyes to the glorious
vistas of heaven and wish we were already there – at times like
these, the Holy Spirit enables us to speak our unspeakable
longings in a way that touches God and nourishes us.

The Greek adjective used here (*alaletos*) does not mean
'totally inexpressible'. There is another word for that (*alalos*
which means 'mute' or 'unable to speak'). What it means is
'unable to be expressed in rational speech'. The phrase occurs in
secular Greek, for example, to describe shared secrets of love. It
does not mean nonsensical speech. There are other words for
that.[3] But it does mean forms of expression that transcend
ordinary language. So the Holy Spirit enables us to intercede in
ways which exceed normal linguistic forms. According to James
Denney, the word does not mean 'unspoken' but it does mean
'unutterable'. He goes on to talk of groanings or sighs that
'baffle words'.[4]

Gordon Fee agrees. He points out that such praying is only
'inarticulate' in the sense that ordinary words of one's native

language are not being used. He stresses that Paul 'certainly does not intend to describe silent praying', a practice which, like silent reading, was rare in biblical times, but praying that transcends one's normal abilities of expression.[5]

Translators have not found it easy to put the phrase into English, although they all throw light on the concept. Here are some of the attempts:

- sighs too deep for words (NRSV, MLB)
- groanings which cannot be uttered (AV, NKJV, NASB)
- groans too deep for words (Cassirer)
- groans that words cannot express (GNB)
- such feeling that it cannot be expressed in words (LB)
- yearnings that can find no words (Weymouth)
- making prayer out of our wordless sighs, our aching groans (Message)
- expresses our pleas in a way that could never be put into words (JB).

In simple terms, even when our human words are embarrassingly weak and ineffective, the Holy Spirit enables us to commune with God. When our hearts cry in anguish, the Spirit lifts us to the Lord. When our minds search fruitlessly for adequate expressions of praise and adoration, the Spirit raises us to unexpected heights.

It is important to note at this point that although Paul describes the Holy Spirit here as interceding **for** us, he is also referring to the Spirit praying **through** us. Murray points out that the use of the plural word 'hearts' makes it plain that the reference is to believers, not the Spirit:

> 'The groanings will have to be understood as the groanings which are registered in the hearts of the children of God. We cannot reasonably think of the Holy Spirit himself, apart from the agency and instrumentality of those on whose behalf he intercedes, as presenting his intercessions to the Father in the form of his own groanings. The reference to the hearts in verse 27 clearly implies that the hearts are those of the children of God. It must be, therefore, in their

hearts that the groanings take place and groanings are those
of the saints. They are, however, the **media** of the Holy
Spirit's intercessions and they ascend to the throne of grace
in the form of groanings.'[6]

All the biblical commentators I have consulted agree with this.
While it is the Spirit who energizes and authenticates our
prayers, they are still ours, even though articulated in the most
simple forms. John Calvin, for example, writes:

> 'Not that he [the Spirit] actually prays or groans but arouses
> in us assurance, desires, and sighs, to conceive which our
> natural powers could scarcely suffice. And Paul, with good
> reason, calls "unspeakable" these groans which believers
> give forth under the guidance of the Spirit...'[7]

In other words, while the utterances are ours, the power is the
Spirit's.

Exactly what Paul means in Romans 8:26–27 will probably
always be unclear. But it certainly covers a wide range of
yearnings and longings for God which may be expressed in
many ways, both rationally and non-rationally, both cognit-
ively and intuitively.

'Searches the hearts'

Now here is the wonderful part. Our heavenly Father searches
our hearts and knows the mind of the Spirit. Furthermore, the
Spirit only prays what is right – He always prays according to
the will of God. Intriguingly, we are often just as ignorant after
the prayer as before, because the Spirit enables us to communicate *'with groans that words cannot express'* (Romans 8:26). But we
do know the Holy Spirit has enabled us to pray well. And so we
experience the peace of God and the reassurance of faith.

At the age of twenty, the young Jonathan Edwards wrote in
his diary:

> 'Resolved, when I find those "groanings which cannot be
> uttered", of which the apostle speaks, and those "breath-
> ings of soul for the longing it hath" of which the psalmist

speaks, Ps 119:20, that I will promote them to the utmost of my power; and that I will not be weary of earnestly endeavouring to vent my desires, nor of the repetitions of such earnestness. July 23 and August 10, 1723.'[8]

Even at this young age, Jonathan Edwards was learning lessons of prayer that would undergird his ministry for years to come. Passion for Christ was a frequent theme of his preaching and writing. Even though we do not know exactly what he experienced in his communion with God, there is no doubt about his determination and commitment. With such resolution, he dedicated himself to uninhibited and unhindered prayer in the Spirit! Little wonder that, a decade later, he was largely instrumental in New England's Great Awakening! It is in the intimacy of spiritual prayer that such a passion is discovered and developed.

When the Holy Spirit invades our prayer, He enables us to pour out to God deep yearnings and unfulfilled aspirations that would otherwise wither like wilted plants.

There are times when all we can do is sigh or literally groan our yearnings to the Lord. When I was in hospital after a near-fatal accident, I was in such a state it was impossible to think clearly, let alone pray clearly. All I could do was groan – but this became a kind of prayer which conveyed more than articulated words might have been able to do. I can recall other occasions when I have simply repeated the name 'Jesus' over and over again. It seemed both the only and the best thing to do. At other times, I have literally sighed out the yearning of my soul to God. Many Christians have similar experiences.

Expressing the inexpressible

It is often argued that there is a reference here to the prayer-gift of speaking in tongues. This beautiful charism enables us to express what normal speech cannot convey. Paul explains that when he speaks in tongues it is his spirit praying (1 Corinthians 14:14). In other words, the prayer rises from the depths of our hearts and brings the yearnings of our souls to God.

In his Homily on Romans 8, the great Chrysostom argues that Paul is referring here to 'a gift of prayer' which has now languished from the Church. He notes elsewhere that this gift was usually associated 'with a tongue'.[9] According to Macchia, a significant number of modern scholars agree.[10] Johannes Behm certainly thinks so and has no hesitation in asserting his view.[11]

There is no doubt that tongue-speaking enables us to express what normal speech cannot convey. In other words, the prayer rises from the depths of our hearts and brings the yearnings of our souls to God. It is possible that what Edwards described may have been an experience of speaking in tongues. Remember, Paul is not talking about yearnings that cannot be expressed at all – but only those desires of the soul which cannot find expression through normal speech.

Certainly, many believers who know nothing of the Greek text or grammatical niceties, believe this is a reference to glossolalia. Those who do pray in tongues usually feel an echo of their experience in this passage. For this is what it seems like. When we don't know how to pray, and our own words are ineffective and inadequate, glossolalia is a wonderful gift.

Paul exhorts us to *'pray without ceasing'* (1 Thessalonians 5:17 NKJV). It is universally understood that he did not intend us to take this literally – in other words, that there are times when it is simply impossible to pray in the strict sense of the word. Generally, Paul's injunction is taken to mean, 'Be in a continual spirit of prayer'. This is a thoroughly sensible and reasonable way to understand the text. When we walk with the Lord, it is possible and, to be honest, essential to develop such an approach. Every moment should be lived in communion with Christ. However, it must also be admitted that prayer in tongues helps us in this endeavour. Because we can pray in tongues instinctively, almost without thinking about it, just as we might hum a well-known tune, we can in reality pray in every disengaged moment when we pray in tongues.

It is possible to develop the habit of praying with the spirit to the degree where we do it automatically at every opportunity – driving the car, waiting for an automated phone message to finish, making a cup of tea, walking between offices, during television commercials, in an airport departure lounge, standing at a train station and so on. No moment is wasted as, without mental effort, we pray continually, with the spirit, in the languages given to us by God.

Struggling with the need of a friend suffering with terminal cancer, a student in one of my classes wrote, 'At times I have had no idea what to pray or what to say to his family. Speaking in tongues takes care of the prayers that I cannot aptly express in my own language and provides me with godly wisdom to say appropriate things to his family during this terrible time.'

Some years ago, Vanessa and I took a seventeen-year-old girl into our home. She lived with us for five years and became like a daughter to us. After a very happy marriage, she was found to have contracted cancer and after a time of intense and prolonged suffering, she died.

Some time later, his eyes shining with wonder, her husband said to my wife and me, 'Helen's whole life was a prayer. She seemed to be praying all the time.'

Then he told us something quite remarkable 'You know,' he said, 'during the last few days she couldn't speak normally at all. But the amazing thing was that she was still able to pray in tongues. You could hardly hear her, but her lips moved gently as she communed with the Lord. Even the nursing staff commented on the fact that although she couldn't talk to anyone else, she could still talk to God in the language He gave her.'

Vanessa and I were deeply moved by this. I began to see how much harder it would have been for her, had she not known how to pray with the spirit. In those last, terrible days of suffering, it was virtually impossible for her to focus her thoughts in any meaningful way. But she could pray in tongues. Because it demanded no intellectual effort, she was able to relax and allow the Holy Spirit to assist her in this wonderful way in her intimacy with her Lord.

This is the most moving example I know of the Spirit of God helping us in our weakness. If I never knew of any other, I would be convinced by this of the value of speaking in tongues. But even in less dramatic circumstances, when we struggle to pray effectively, it is good to know the Spirit is there with us helping us in our time of need.

Don't forget

- Strangely enough, although what we need to do most is to pray, this is the very thing that in ourselves we cannot do! We depend utterly on the Holy Spirit to help us.

- When our human words are embarrassingly weak and ineffective, the Holy Spirit enables us to commune with God. When our hearts cry in anguish, the Spirit lifts us to the Lord. When our minds search fruitlessly for adequate expressions of praise and adoration, the Spirit raises us to unexpected heights.

- The Spirit only prays what is right – He always prays according to the will of God.

- When the Holy Spirit invades our prayer, He enables us to pour out to God deep yearnings and unfulfilled aspirations that would otherwise wither like wilted plants.

- When we don't know how to pray, and our own words are ineffective and inadequate, glossolalia is a wonderful gift.

Notes

1 NRSV.
2 F. Macchia, 'Sighs Too Deep for Words' in *Journal of Pentecostal Theology* 1 (October 1992), p. 62.
3 For example, 'babble' (Matthew 6:7); 'babbler' (Acts 17:18); 'nonsense' (Luke 24:11).
4 James Denney, 'St Paul's Epistle to the Romans' in *The Expositor's Greek Testament*, Vol. II (Grand Rapids: Eerdmans, 1967), p. 651.
5 G. Fee, *Listening to the Spirit in the Text* (Grand Rapids: Eerdmans, 2000), p. 112; G. Fee, *God's Empowering Presence: the Holy Spirit in the Letters of Paul* (Peabody, Mass.: Henrickson, 1994), pp. 581ff.
6 J. Murray, *The Epistle to the Romans* (Grand Rapids: Eerdmans, 1973), p. 312.
7 John Calvin, *Institutes*, III, 5.
8 J. Edwards, *The Religious Affections* (Edinburgh: The Banner of Truth Trust, [1746] 1984), p. xxii.
9 John Chrysostom, *Homilies on Romans*, 14; *Homilies on 1 Corinthians* 35.
10 Macchia, 'Sighs Too Deep for Words', p. 59.
11 J. Behm, 'Parakaleo' in G. Friedrich (ed.), *Theological Dictionary of the New Testament* (Grand Rapids: Eerdmans, 1968), p. 813.

Chapter 13

'My Spirit Prays'
(1 Corinthians 14:14)

Prayer with the spirit means praying in tongues

The phrase 'pray in the Spirit' has become very popular as a result of the widespread Pentecostal and Charismatic revival. Although it includes many crucial aspects of prayer, as we have seen, often it is associated only with speaking in tongues. That's fine for charismatics, but non-charismatics are justly concerned at the implication that their prayers may be seen as somehow inferior.

'How can anyone pray a true prayer at all without the presence of the Holy Spirit?' one man once challenged me. It's a good question.

In the original Greek text, it is not easy to distinguish between the words 'spirit' and 'Spirit'. There is no parallel to the English use of capitals. Only the context enables us to decide whether the human spirit or the Holy Spirit is intended. So some New Testament passages clearly describe the work of the Holy Spirit, while others could be seen as a reference to the cry of the human spirit to God as ignited by the Holy Spirit. It is the context that helps us to decide. Gordon Fee acknowledges the ambiguity by using the term 'S/spirit'.[1] This is a very important issue.

Glossolalia is prayer with the spirit

There is one form of prayer referred to in the New Testament which is specifically designated as prayer of the human spirit –

and this is glossolalia or praying in tongues. Paul makes this point in his first letter to the Corinthians, where he compares and contrasts praying with the understanding with praying with the spirit:

> *'For if I pray in a tongue, my spirit prays, but my mind is unfruitful. So what shall I do? I will pray with my spirit, but I will also pray with my mind; I will sing with my spirit, but I will also sing with my mind.'*   (1 Corinthians 14:14–16)

There is no question that Paul here equates praying with the human spirit with praying in tongues. Just as prayer in our own language is praying with the mind, so praying in a tongue is praying with the spirit.

This is not the same thing as praying **in** the Holy Spirit, although it is part of it. The latter encompasses every kind of true prayer. Praying **with** the human spirit is exclusively praying in tongues. Arthur Wallis brings out this distinction very plainly in his excellent book *Pray in the Spirit*:

> 'It is necessary to define our terms as there has been a tendency in some quarters to assume too readily that praying in the Spirit and praying with the spirit are identical terms ... Failing to distinguish the two terms, some have concluded that praying in the Spirit is limited to praying in tongues ... Expressed in the most practical terms it means that the Holy Spirit inspires, guides, energizes and sustains the praying.'[2]

Budgen argues that both praying with the spirit and praying with the mind are intellectually meaningful.[3] He quotes passages like *'Jesus knew in his spirit that this was what they were thinking in their hearts'* (Mark 2:8), *'The spirit is willing, but the body is weak'* (Matthew 26:41) and Paul's *'spirit was provoked within him'* to see that the city was full of idols (Acts 17:16 NKJB). If anything, these passages prove the opposite. The spirit can be stirred or moved or angered, as Paul's was, beyond rational language or intellectual understanding. Such experiences often lie too deep for words. But they are important and significant, none the less. Or putting it differently, an experience may be meaningful either spiritually, emotionally or intellectually – and all are equally valid. Prayer with the spirit is not meaningless. But the meaning lies deeper than logic or reason. To use contemporary terms, it is right-brained rather than left-brained, intuitive rather than cognitive.

An innate ability?

It is interesting to raise the question: is the ability to pray with the spirit actually an innate human ability? In other words, had human beings not sinned, would it always have been possible to pray in tongues? Is glossolalia a natural communication skill which has been lost to us because of the lethal power of sin?

Outside of Christ, we are dead in our transgressions and sins – a fact which Paul repeats with double emphasis in his letter to the Ephesians (2:1, 5). We are cut off from God and unable to communicate with Him spiritually. The language of the spirit is rendered silent because the spirit itself is shrouded in silence. Deadened by sin and numbed by iniquity, it is no longer able to express itself.

In Christ, however, we have been made alive (Ephesians 2:5). Although it is difficult to find New Testament references which explicitly state that regeneration means the regeneration of the spirit (normally it is 'we' who are made alive), it is fair to conclude that this new life is spiritual. There is no physical or intellectual change: our bodies remain the same, but spiritually it is springtime: new life is blossoming forth. The human spirit is brought back from the dead. It is no longer silent. It has once again been given voice.

So Frederic Rendall writes:

> 'The spirit of man owes its original existence to the quickening inspiration of the Holy Spirit, and depends for its continued life on the constant supply of life-giving power: its impulses are therefore purely spiritual.'[4]

Paul puts it like this:

> *'But if Christ is in you, your body is dead because of sin, yet your spirit is alive because of righteousness. And if the Spirit of him*

> *who raised Jesus from the dead is living in you, he who raised*
> *Christ from the dead will also give life to your mortal bodies*
> *through his Spirit, who lives in you.'*   (Romans 8:10–11)

The body is still subject to decay. But the spirit now lives. The day is coming when our dying bodies will also come to life, but till then they are inanimate and inert. The spirit, however, has now been regenerated and revived.

James Denney expresses this very clearly:

> 'The body, it cannot be denied, is dead because of sin: the experience we call death is inevitable for it ... but the spirit (i.e. the human spirit, as is shown by the contrast with *soma* [the flesh]) is life, God-begotten, God-sustained life...' [5]

So, if it is right to suggest that the ability to pray in a tongue is an innate human ability, then this ability is actually restored in Christ.

All it needs now is for the Holy Spirit to be poured out upon us to reactivate that lost talent. When the Holy Spirit comes, He enables us again to express ourselves through glossolalia. Praying in tongues, then, is the restored cry of a human spirit brought back to life by the Spirit of God through the redemption that is in Christ Jesus. This is a great encouragement to people who have asked God to enable them to pray in tongues but without any apparent result. When we think of glossolalia as a gift we have to drag down from heaven or somehow pull in from some external realm, we can easily be discouraged. But when we think of it as a capacity lying dormant within us, needing only to be awakened by the Holy Spirit, our faith can rise up more readily. Paul makes it plain that when he speaks in tongues it is **his** spirit that is praying (1 Corinthians 14:14). Such prayers rise up from within us.

As long as we think of glossolalia as 'the **gift** of tongues', we are tempted to believe that only some people may receive this 'gift' and, hence, it is not for us. There are many who have adopted this position. They say things like, 'If God wants to give it to me, He will.' But in reality, they have probably adopted a position where they have ceased to expect it. In some ways, this takes the pressure off. If I believe that glossolalia is only for certain believers, this comforts me and removes the motivation from me to seek to do it. If, on the other hand, I believe that I can pray in tongues, and this is God's will for me, I will continue to reach out for it. It is interesting to note that the phrase 'gift of tongues' cannot be found in Scripture. The New Testament only uses expressions like 'speak' or 'pray' in tongues. In the list of spiritual gifts in 1 Corinthians 12, the term is *'different kinds of tongues'*. The emphasis is on the speaking not the receiving.

It has been argued that Paul's rhetorical question, *'Do all speak in tongues?'* (1 Corinthians 12:30) shows that glossolalia is not for everyone. However, the context makes it plain that Paul is referring to public utterances of tongues in gatherings of believers, not to personal or private speaking. Given that tongue-speech is clearly a form of prayer, it seems hard to accept that it is not possible for every believer to practise it.

Bittlinger writes, 'Psychologically the only explanation that satisfies me is the fact that this [glossolalia] is a potential capacity, dormant in most people, awakened in the Christian by the Holy Spirit and filled with meaning'.[6] Reformed scholar Vern Poythress is inclined to agree. 'It seems,' he writes, 'that the capacity for free vocalization is a normal, God-given capacity'.[7] Linguist Chris Kenneally describes glossolalia as 'a universal human experience'.[8] Researcher Virginia Hine expresses a similar opinion.[9] William Samarin suggests that human beings have a natural language-creating ability. He describes tongue-speech as 'an expression of the ineffable'.[10]

Ken Chant argues that the ability to speak in a tongue is 'aroused' or 'induced' by the Holy Spirit. He rejects the word 'imparted' on the grounds that the ability to exercise glossolalia is a natural human ability which the coming of the Spirit awakens, not a supernatural ability given by the Spirit.[11]

Glossolalia is 'elevated discourse'

This helps to explain Luke's wording in his explanation of the Pentecost story:

> *'All of them were filled with the Holy Spirit and began to speak in other tongues as the Spirit enabled them.'* (Acts 2:4)

Luke is careful to point out that it was the disciples, not the Holy Spirit, who spoke in tongues. What the Spirit of God did was to 'enable' them to speak. The New Revised Standard Version says the Spirit *'gave them ability'*. The Holy Spirit does not speak in tongues. We do. We cannot do it without the Spirit's help; the Spirit will not do it without our co-operation.

Luke's phrase *'as the Spirit enabled them'* includes a verb which occurs only twice elsewhere in the New Testament – in reference to Peter's Pentecost sermon (Acts 2:14) and Paul's defence before Agrippa (Acts 26:25). It describes noble or exalted language. The term was used in ancient times of a poet or an inspired singer. It was not gibberish or wild babbling. Thayer describes it as referring to 'dignified and elevated discourse . . . ' and says it was used of wise men and philosophers. Chrysostom (347–407), the 'Golden-mouth', Bishop of Antioch and Constantinople, says the apostles spoke 'profound utterances . . . the things they spoke were wonderful'.[12]

Clearly, the languages used by the apostles were out of the ordinary. Their ability to so speak was given by the Spirit of God. Yet, at the same time, it was they who spoke, not the Spirit.

To pray with the human spirit is to pray in tongues. But the spirit cannot pray at all unless the Holy Spirit makes it possible.

Don't forget

- Praying in tongues is the restored cry of a human spirit brought back to life by the Spirit of God through the redemption that is in Christ Jesus.

- Given that tongue-speech is clearly a form of prayer, it seems hard to accept that it is not possible for every believer to practise it.

- The Holy Spirit does not speak in tongues. We do. We cannot do it without the Spirit's help; the Spirit will not do it without our co-operation.

Notes

1 G. Fee, *God's Empowering Presence: the Holy Spirit in the Letters of Paul* (Peabody, Mass.: Henrickson, 1994), pp. 24ff.

2 A. Wallis, *Pray in the Spirit* (Victory Press, 1975), pp. 23ff.

3 V. Budgen, *The Charismatics and the Word of God* (Welwyn: Evangelical Press, 1986), p. 52.

4 F. Rendall, 'The Epistle to the Galatians' in W.R. Nicholl (ed.), *The Expositor's Greek Testament Volume III* (Grand Rapids: Eerdmans, 1967), p. 186.

5 J. Denney, 'St Paul's Epistle to the Romans' in Nicholl (ed.), *The Expositor's Greek Testament*, Vol. II, p. 646.

6 A. Bittlinger, *Gifts and Graces* (London: Hodder and Stoughton, 1967), p. 100.

7 V. Poythress in W. Mills (ed.), *Speaking in Tongues: A Guide to Research in Glossolalia* (Grand Rapids: Eerdmans, 1986), p. 473.

8 C. Kenneally, *Other Tongues*, unpublished thesis (University of Melbourne, 1990), p. 10.

9 V. Hine in W. Mills (ed.), *Speaking in Tongues*, p. 460.

10 W. Samarin in W. Mills (ed.), *Speaking in Tongues*, p. 453.

11 K. Chant, *Clothed with Power* (Kingswood, NSW: Ken Chant Ministries, 1993), p. 114.

12 John Chrysostom, *Homily 4*.

Chapter 14

'Edifies Himself'
(1 Corinthians 14:4)

Prayer with the spirit builds us up

To pray in a tongue, it is necessary to be filled with the Spirit. In every biblical record we have of people's initial speaking in tongues, it always happens as the result of the outpouring of the Holy Spirit. This was obviously the case at Pentecost (Acts 2:4). It was also true of Saul of Tarsus (Acts 9:17; 1 Corinthians 14:18) and the household of Cornelius (Acts 10:44ff.). It seems a valid assumption that the first Samaritan believers experienced glossolalia – and with them, too, it was the result of the impartation of the Holy Spirit (Acts 8:14–24).[1] A similar conclusion can be drawn in regard to the Corinthians (Acts 18:1ff.), to whom the gospel was preached with signs and wonders (2 Corinthians 12:12) and most of whom practised glossolalia.

This was certainly the situation in Ephesus, where the record plainly says,

> *'When Paul placed his hands on them, the Holy Spirit came on them, and they spoke in tongues and prophesied.'* (Acts 19:6)

In fact, in this case, the enclitic particle used implies an intimate connection between the coming of the Spirit and the resultant glossolalia. We could actually translate it like this:

> 'When Paul placed his hands on them, the Holy Spirit came on them, **and so** they spoke in tongues and prophesied.'

To be filled with the Spirit of God is clearly a prerequisite to speaking in tongues. So it also stands to reason that the more the Holy Spirit fills us, the more effectively we shall pray Spirit-infused prayers.

It is recognized that forms of glossolalia also occur in non-Christian contexts. But this does not alter the fact that **Christian** glossolalia is activated by the Holy Spirit. It is both the context and the content that are the issue. A similar point might be made about prophesying, especially when foretelling the future, which also occurs in both Christian and non-Christian settings.

Spiritual strengthening

Naturally, prayer with the spirit is edifying – it builds us up (1 Corinthians 14:4). In other words, when we pray in this way, we are restored and renewed inwardly. Similarly, Jude links the concept of praying in the Holy Spirit with the idea of being built up in faith (Jude 20).

A spiritual strengthening occurs when we pray with the spirit. At times when prayer seems laborious, an infusion of spiritual power can turn it into a time of refreshing in the presence of the Lord. We begin in weakness, but we conclude in strength; we cry out in depression, but we are answered in triumph; we seek the Lord in frailty, but we find Him in power.

The question is often asked, 'How can praying with the spirit be helpful if you don't understand what you are saying?' This is a fair question, but it misses the point of prayer with the spirit. It is spiritually, not intellectually, beneficial.

A similar point might be made about music. Even someone who knows nothing at all about music theory or musical instruments can be affected by a moving melody or a stirring rhapsody. Martial music usually arouses feelings of national pride or Christian fervour. Romantic music, by contrast, tends to make us sentimental or soft-hearted. When we hear a song with a lively beat, our spirits are lifted and maybe our toes start tapping. In plain terms, music can communicate a strong and effective message, but it is through the senses, rather than the intellect. Its therapeutic value remains.

When we pray with the spirit, something similar happens. Although we may have little cerebral understanding of what is being said, we may still benefit emotionally, spiritually and even physically.

In our modern, westernized world, we like to think that everything we do is logical and reasonable. This is, of course, a huge self-deception. Most people's lives are influenced by their emotions and feelings more than their intellects. Music, sport, sex, pleasure, possessions, popularity – these are the things that motivate us most of the time. But we still like to see ourselves as thoughtful, civilized human beings who have long since abandoned primitive practices and whose lives are controlled by sensible, rational decision-making.

So the idea of being helped by something as simple and old-fashioned as praying in tongues is offensive to us. It ought not to be. It is a God-given mechanism which enables the Holy Spirit to penetrate the depths of our being and which makes it possible for us to break through into the realm of the Spirit.

Jackie Pullinger is well known for her courageous pioneering social work in the slums of Hong Kong. In 1966, she went there as a young, single woman, without any backing or official support, because she felt God had called her to reach out with His love to the thousands of poor, hungry and suffering dwellers of what was then called the Walled City.

In her own lifetime, her story has become one of the classics of missionary endeavour. She has been acclaimed, even by secular media, as a legend in Hong Kong.

In her book *Chasing the Dragon*, Pullinger tells how the one thing that really helped her to keep going was the gift of a prayer language. She recalls how she got started with this kind of intimacy with God. This is what she says:

> 'Every day ... I prayed in the language of the Spirit. Fifteen minutes by the clock. I still felt it to be an exercise. Before praying in the Spirit, I said, "Lord, I don't know how to pray, or whom to pray for. Will You pray through me – and will You lead me to the people who want You." And I would begin my fifteen-minute stint.
>
> After about six weeks I noticed something remarkable. Those I talked to about Christ believed. I could not understand it at first and wondered how my Chinese had so suddenly improved, or if I had stumbled on a splendid new

evangelistic technique. But I was saying the same things as before. It was some time before I realized what had changed. This time I was talking about Jesus to people who wanted to hear. I had let God have a hand in my prayers and it produced a direct result. Instead of my deciding what I wanted to do for God and asking His blessing I was asking Him to do His will through me as I prayed in the language He gave me.'[2]

Elsewhere, she writes of the overwhelming weariness and strain that came upon her as she had to keep going night and day to respond to the needs of the Walled City. Sometimes, she was so exhausted, she could hardly think, let alone pray. At these times, as she stumbled through the filthy lanes or collapsed on her bed after hours of ministry, all she could do was pray in the Spirit. This provided her with the strength she needed.

Releasing the unconscious

It is years now since Sigmund Freud suggested that there were different levels in our minds – the conscious, the preconscious (i.e. subconscious) and the unconscious.[3] In the conscious level are those thoughts which we are actually thinking at any given time. In the subconscious level lies a great store of facts and ideas that we can draw upon at any time and bring into consciousness. This is what we commonly call the memory.

In the unconscious are many ideas, thoughts, facts, events and experiences which, by contrast, it is impossible to call into the conscious level. They are too deeply buried. Nevertheless, argued Freud, they can still have a great influence on the way we live now. Psychiatry attempts to unlock the unconscious mind and unmask such experiences and thereby remove their power.

But what if the memories are released, but still haunt us? What if, even worse, once they are exposed, they actually become more of a problem? Furthermore, even if, through therapy, dark memories are extracted from the unconscious, how can we be sure they are **all** released? What can we do about those that never surface, but still go on affecting us?

This is where prayer with the spirit may be wonderfully therapeutic! What we do not know, the Holy Spirit does know. Where we are ignorant, the Holy Spirit is fully informed!

Could it be that when we pray in tongues, the Holy Spirit is dredging out of our lives black shades from the past and releasing us from their debilitating and negative influences? That painful unconscious memories are being exhumed from our hearts? That negative, hindering emotions are being hosed away? It may be objected that I am reading too much into the passage, and perhaps I am, but from a pastoral perspective, there seems much to commend this concept. From many years of observation in the ministry, I know that when people have prayed their way through spiritual blockages and psychopathological difficulties by speaking in tongues, they have broken through far quicker than they would have done through long times of even the best counselling.

Undoubtedly, as someone has put it, the Holy Spirit knows all about us from the womb to the tomb. So if anyone is able to uncover and wash out hurts and injuries long buried in the past, it is He.

So,

> ' . . . the Spirit helps us in our weakness. We do not know what we ought to pray for, but the Spirit himself intercedes for us with groans that words cannot express. And he who searches our hearts knows the mind of the Spirit, because the Spirit intercedes for the saints in accordance with God's will.'
>
> (Romans 8:26–27)

Jesus indicated something similar when He said:

> ' "If anyone is thirsty, let him come to me and drink. Whoever believes in me, as the Scripture has said, streams of living water will flow from within him." By this he meant the Spirit, whom those who believed in him were later to receive. Up to that time the Spirit had not been given, since Jesus had not yet been glorified.'
>
> (John 7:37–39)

The phrase translated 'from within him' here means literally 'from the stomach'! There is a strong suggestion of the infilling of the Holy Spirit affecting us deeply – and even physically – and releasing a flow of life. I believe too little attention has been given to this. Praying with the spirit is a spiritual therapy. There is a life-flow here that is transforming!

Some years ago, I was struggling with worry over an incident that had occurred involving another brother on our staff. I couldn't seem to shake it off. One morning as I was out walking and talking with the Lord, I felt as if the Holy Spirit said to me, 'Pray it out! Pray it out!'

I took this as a word from the Lord and began to speak earnestly and consistently in a Spirit-given prayer language. I did this for about twenty minutes and, as I did so, the concern I felt lifted and my spirit felt free and refreshed. The worry disappeared. Today I cannot remember what the problem was. Praying in the Spirit is a marvellous way of cleansing and flushing the system from past obstructions and contaminations.

Counselling is a valid and honoured aspect of Christian pastoral care whose value is being increasingly recognized. There are times when we need the loving, sensitive care of another brother or sister in Christ. None the less, even the best counselling cannot exhume the problems that sometimes lie buried deep within us. But the Holy Spirit can. Glossolalia is a gift God has provided which penetrates deeper than any human skill can do. There seems little doubt that if more of us prayed more often in tongues for more time, there would be less trauma in our lives. There is a therapeutic value in glossolalia that deserves greater recognition. In simple terms, speaking in tongues is good for us. Or to use biblical language, when we speak in tongues we are edified (1 Corinthians 14:4).

Don't forget

- When we pray with the spirit, although we may have little cerebral understanding of what is being said, we may still benefit emotionally, spiritually and even physically.
- The Holy Spirit knows all about us from the womb to the tomb. So if anyone is able to uncover and wash out hurts and injuries long buried in the past, it is He.

- Praying with the spirit is a spiritual therapy. There is a life-flow here that is transforming!

- Glossolalia is a gift God has provided which penetrates deeper than any human skill can do.

- If we prayed more often in tongues for more time, there would be less trauma in our lives.

- Speaking in tongues is good for us. Or to use biblical language, when we speak in tongues we are edified (1 Corinthians 14:4).

Notes

1   See A. Barnes, *Notes on the New Testament* (Chicago: Moody, 1968), pp. 430f.; R.J. Knowling, 'The Acts of the Apostles' in W.R. Nicholl (ed.), *The Expositor's Greek Testament* (Grand Rapids: Eerdmans, 1967), pp. 261ff.

2   J. Pullinger, *Chasing the Dragon* (London: Hodder and Stoughton, 1983), pp. 62f.; *The Crack in the Wall: the life and death of Kowloon Walled City* (London: Hodder and Stoughton, 1989).

3   S. Freud, 'The Unconscious' in *Great Books of the Western World Volume 54, Freud* (Encyclopaedia Britannica, 1952), pp. 428ff.

Chapter 15

'Rivers of Living Water'
(John 7:37)[1]

*It is refreshing to express our prayers in words
given by the Spirit*

One of the great values of prayer in tongues is that it enables us
to pray when we don't know how to pray! Putting it differently,
where human language fails, the language of the Spirit succeeds.

This is especially true of times of petition or supplication.
Often, we are only too well aware of a problem or difficulty, but
how should we pray? What is the best answer? What is the will
of God? What should we ask for? What is the best outcome?
When we use this prayer-gift, it is reassuring to understand that
the Spirit knows the answers to all these questions and is
interceding *'for the saints* [us] *in accordance with God's will'*
(Romans 8:27).

'A burden in prayer'

When I was a young Christian, people used to talk about having
'a burden in prayer'. By this, they meant that they felt a kind of
heaviness, almost a physical pressure, like a great, soft weight
on their shoulders, as the urgency or gravity of a problem or
need was picked up through prayer. Then they would bring it to
God, pouring out their hearts through glossolalia until the
burden lifted and they felt a sense of peace. The answer was
on its way!

I am sure many people have the same experience today, although the terminology may have changed. There are times when we bow before the Lord and there is a kind of gentle but firm restraint upon us to remain longer in prayer. Of course, we are always free to stop whenever we like, as God never forces us to pray. But, nevertheless, He has a way of holding us before Him until we have accomplished the purpose of the prayer. I know I myself have on many occasions got off my knees or out of my chair thinking, 'That will do', only to find myself praying more. It actually feels as if the Lord has gently placed His hands on my shoulders and eased me back down again. I think there is a sensitivity to God in this area that we need to cultivate. I wonder how often we miss the purposes of God because we simply do not give enough time to waiting on Him.

It is noteworthy that Paul orders us to pray on all occasions with *'all kinds of prayers and requests'* (Ephesians 6:18), which allows for pleading before God in many ways – with sighs, with tears, with groaning, with words in our own language and with those given to us by the Holy Spirit.

Even more, He tells us that when we **do** pray, we should do so *'in the Spirit'*. In the New Revised Standard Version rendering of this text, Paul urges us to pray *'at all times in every prayer and supplication'*. In other words, no matter what the need at the time, or the form of the prayer, it is pointless to pray if we don't do it *'in the Spirit'*. As we have seen, this means more than just speaking in tongues, but it certainly includes tongues.

Bringing our requests to God is limited if we exclude tongues from our form of prayer. On the other hand, tongue-speaking adds enormous strength and depth to prayers of petition. When humanly we are at a loss for words, the Spirit comes to our aid and helps us to intercede according to the will of God.

This is also true of praise. How feeble and struggling are our attempts to praise God adequately. How stumbling are our words and how shallow our phrases. Of course, it is proper that we worship God in our own language to the best of our ability. But like Charles Wesley, we are constantly frustrated with our human limitations and we cry in desperation, 'O for a thousand tongues to sing my great Redeemer's praise!'

It is refreshing and exciting at such times to express our adoration in words given by the Spirit – words which flow freely and fluently as the Spirit empowers us. This is what happened at Pentecost. They all spoke in tongues as the Spirit enabled them and in doing so declared the *'wonders of God'* in a way they could never have done on their own (Acts 2:1–11).

Music and song

Prayer with the spirit also contains a hint of music or song. In his letter to the Corinthians, Paul clearly and closely connects both praying and singing with the spirit (1 Corinthians 14:15). Such communion with God is unquestionably beneficial.

His reference to *'psalms, hymns and spiritual songs'* (Ephesians 5:19; Colossians 3:16) is also interesting. We know what psalms and hymns are. But what about spiritual songs? Are they just something like the 'choruses' we might sing today? Or are they forms of music in which the presence of the Holy Spirit is especially felt? The fact that in the letter to the Ephesians the statement is preceded by an injunction to be filled with the Spirit (5:18) adds weight to this proposition. Further, Paul goes on to say that we sing these songs with *charis* in our hearts. This word means 'grace' but may suggest connotations of charismata as well.

Thus, if we link the phrase 'spiritual songs' with Paul's reference in his letter to the Corinthians to 'singing with the spirit' (14:14, 15), it seems obvious that spiritual songs are harmonies inspired by the Spirit and sung in the language of the Spirit – in other words, speaking in tongues. The context of 1 Corinthians 14:14 is also that of thanksgiving. In the following verses, the words 'praise', 'thanksgiving' and 'give thanks' all occur in quick succession.

There is an intriguing ambiguity here. When Paul enjoins us to be *'filled with the Spirit'*, he uses phraseology which could equally be rendered 'be filled in spirit'. The verb 'fill' is not followed, as it usually is, by a Greek genitive (cf. Acts 2:4; 4:31; 9:17) but by a prepositional phrase beginning with 'in'.

This grammatical form is normally used of the Holy Spirit (Ephesians 6:18; Jude 20) but can be used of the human spirit (1 Corinthians 14:16). So we are faced with a question. Is Paul telling us to be filled with the Spirit of God? Or is this an injunction to be sure that our own spirits are 'full'? In some respects, the question is academic, as the result in either case is the indwelling and infilling of the Holy Spirit (1 Corinthians 6:19f.; Ephesians 2:21f.).

There are additional hints of glossolalia in Colossians 3:16–17. Not only is the phrase 'spiritual songs' used, but these songs originate *'in your hearts'* – which may well be a synonym for 'spirits'.

Furthermore, the passage begins with a reference to the *logos* or 'word' of Christ. This is normally taken to mean the teaching or preaching of Christ, which is clearly its obvious meaning. However, as the word *logos* also occurs in the context of spiritual gifts (Acts 8:21; 1 Corinthians 12:8), there could be a secondary suggestion of Spirit-enabled speech as well. Certainly the whole passage has a charismatic ring about it.

In Philippians 3:3, Paul uses the phrase 'worship in the Spirit'. Again, this could be translated 'with the (human?) spirit'. If so, there is a suggestion here of glossolalia. Sometimes, it is difficult to worship with our limited vocabulary. Unless we are specially gifted with language skills, meaningful worship is not an easy task. We can find some words with which to praise the Lord, but before long we may seem to be repeating ourselves. So we finish up saying something like, 'Dear Lord, I worship You, hallelujah, for You are holy, praise the Lord, hallelujah, I love You, Lord, hallelujah, oh bless God, praise You, Lord, thank You, Lord, for all Your love and grace, praise God, amen, hallelujah, holy, holy, holy, Lord, praise You, Lord, You are so great, You are so awesome, I worship Your majesty, hallelujah, amen, praise You, Lord...' Surely God must grow bored with such repetitions.

There is obviously a sound argument for reading thoughtful and well-prepared prayers! On the other hand, some people feel that such prayers may also become either stilted or repetitious.

To worship in a tongue makes all the difference. Here the Holy Spirit gives us the words to use and they flow easily and freely like tumbling rivers of praise (John 7:37–39). This is not just a pleasant thing for us – it is also powerful. There is great victory in praising God. Many times the Scriptures affirm this. For instance, when Paul and Silas were in prison in Philippi, it was as they sang hymns of praise to God that they were supernaturally released (Acts 16:25ff.).

The psalmist claims that God is actually enthroned on the praises of His people (Psalm 22:3). And he clearly links praise with the power of God in Psalm 59:

'But I will sing of your strength,
  in the morning I will sing of your love;
for you are my fortress,
  my refuge in times of trouble.
O my Strength, I sing praise to you;
  you, O God, are my fortress, my loving God.'

(Psalm 59:16–17)

To quote Philippians 3:3 again, we have the wonderful opportunity to 'worship in the Spirit'. Not only does it honour God – but it does something for us, too!

Time with God

Sometimes, people claim that they get little out of glossolalia. Clinical experience suggests that this is likely to be the case if we only speak in tongues for short periods. To use an analogy, fitness experts claim that for our bodies to benefit from walking, we need to do it for at least twenty minutes at a time. It takes this long for the heartbeat to rise, for oxygen to flow through the system and so on. Shorter bursts of exercise may actually be of little benefit. I believe a similar principle applies to prayer. Whether in our own language or the language of the Spirit, we need to spend time with God. Certainly, for prayer in tongues to be edifying, it is necessary to linger longer before the Lord. As we commune with Him in loving attendance, the true depths of spiritual communion begin to be explored. It takes time for the human spirit to express itself fully and openly to the Lord.

In recent years, I have adopted a practice of requiring students in one of my classes to commit themselves to the practice of praying in tongues for ten minutes a day for five days a week during the course of the semester. At the end of this period, they have to write a report. Initially, many either found the exercise difficult or felt they were just doing it because it was required, not because it was voluntary. But as they persevered, most of them reported wonderful blessings. In fact, the results have been astonishing.

Jane [2] told how she had many blocks to overcome and could not do the exercise until her fears were resolved. 'The days I least felt like praying in tongues,' she said, 'were the times I most needed it and from this I learned the value of discipline and not giving in to moods or emotions.'

Marilyn found the assignment difficult because she could not see any intellectual value in what she was doing. But the struggle allowed the Holy Spirit to reveal her need to repent and hand it all over to the Lord. As she prayed more, she lost the necessity to feel she had to prove herself. The more this happened the more she could pray in tongues. It was an upward spiral.

Maureen lost the problems she had previously experienced with disturbed sleep. Kay found that while she prayed she would often feel prompted by the Spirit to pray in her mind for a particular person, situation or event. Then she found that during the day she was 'drawn to the Spirit's voice'. Because it was now clearer she was able to listen, discern and act upon it.

Many students reported a greater peace and contentment as a result. The problem was, said Michael, that, as with any prayer, ten minutes was inadequate. 'It is only after half an hour,' he reported, 'that I can start feeling really close to God.'

Lorraine noted that on a few occasions, especially when she did not feel like praying, she had a sense of God's love, majesty and greatness. She struggled to find the words to describe how she felt. 'When times have been tough,' she said, 'just praising God, even when I do not know what I am saying or I don't know what to say, has given me a sense of peace and knowledge that God is in control of every situation.'

Even those who had been walking in the Spirit for many years found the exercise challenging. Ben enjoyed praying in tongues but

'Within the first few days of beginning this prayer exercise, I found myself confronted with a terrible thing: my own lack of prayerfulness. It came as a shock to me to realize that deliberately setting aside ten minutes to pray in tongues was far more difficult than I imagined it would be. I lost concentration very rapidly and I was far too restless, allowing my thoughts to wander and being slow to direct my mind and heart back to God. This prayer exercise made me realize that my prayerfulness and perhaps even my attitude to God and to being disciplined had become sloppy. I've had to humble myself before the Lord and call upon Him in a new and fresh way.'

The discipline of praying regularly with the Spirit was illustrated by Andrew's comment that he initially found the exercise difficult because he thought that much of what he was doing was 'in the flesh'. However, 'looking back,' he wrote, 'I can see the benefits of the exercise and I intend on continuing in my own devotions. It was like putting my faith into action as I spoke aloud and I was able to sense the presence of God in my life in a more tangible way.'

Beverley felt uncomfortable and embarrassed when she first began to speak in tongues. She admitted this to God and told Him she was willing to do it anyway. She persevered but still did not feel particularly spiritual or godly. Since then, she reported, 'the value of praying with the spirit has been both surprising and profound.' The results included peace, calmness, spiritual insight, spiritual growth, greater intimacy with Jesus, more effective prayer and a positive change in her general temperament, after a bout of sickness.

Colin was delighted with the benefits. 'Firstly,' he said without any qualification, 'it revolutionized my prayer life.' He found a greater appreciation of the character and nature of God and saw intercessions for others being answered in a significant way. He gained new insights into Scripture, witnessed more effectively and became bolder in exercising other spiritual gifts.

May was thrilled that people were noticing a difference in her attitude to things and that when she spent time with the Lord she just didn't want to stop. Lorene reported 'an overwhelming feeling of contentment' – the Lord was so close she felt as if she could reach out and touch Him. Interestingly, while she was praying with the spirit, she found her mind actually became clearer and her praying more purposeful.

Matt stated that God's loving kindness was more real to him and that praying in tongues strengthened him in times of spiritual warfare. Gary realized he had been used to feeding his flesh, but not his spirit. This exercise redressed the balance and while he prayed in tongues, God opened his eyes relating to his lifestyle. He also felt a greater compassion for the needy.

Ivan struggled with the normal doubts – 'is it just me making it up?' – and distractions, but when he actually undertook this exercise, 'somehow' his will was under control and he was better able to resist the temptation to think of other things. What he described as a 'thread-bare' Christian life was being lifted to a better level.

Initially, Judy found the exercise a tough one. 'What seemed like ten minutes,' she said, 'was in fact only one or two.' But by the end of the assignment, she found the ten minutes stretching into twenty or thirty. The greatest benefit was a 'much closer relationship' with the Lord Jesus Christ and a deeper sense of worship.

Sue admitted that since being immersed in the Spirit two years previously, she had been too analytical in her approach to tongues and she 'did not understand the priceless value of the gift.' When she began the exercise, she was beset with doubts and cried out to God for reassurance. She heard, almost audibly, the words, 'The righteous shall live by faith.' The doubts broke and she experienced a sense of release and 'wonderful peace'.

Karen testified to increasing confidence; Sally grew less anxious and headaches lessened; Ian became 'more spiritual in the right sense of the word'. Brett found his ability to worship enhanced; God began to reveal things to Cynthia about her personal life while she prayed; Martin wrote, 'It sent my spirit soaring' and increased his passion for Jesus.

Vadi discovered an exciting ability to pray in more languages than she had done previously. And she became more peaceful when she spoke in tongues while driving. 'It is hard to be angry at other drivers when you are praying with the spirit,' she said.

Diana wrote, 'I have noticed subtle changes in some of my attitudes and perceptions.' She also began to pray in tongues in a wider variety of situations, especially at times when prayer seemed difficult. 'I feel more strongly than ever the value of tongues,' she said.

All these testimonies bear witness to the value of praying with the spirit on a regular basis.

Dr David Yonggi Cho is renowned the world over for his remarkable ministry in Korea. It is often claimed that he prays for two or three hours every day. In a ministers' seminar some years ago, he was asked about this. He replied that he did spend long periods in prayer, but, he said, 'the only way I can do this is by praying in tongues. Without the Spirit's help, it is impossible.'

We must pray with the spirit. As we have seen, this is only possible with the help of the Holy Spirit. And when the Spirit does invade our prayers, they are transformed!

Don't forget

- One of the great values of prayer in tongues is that it enables us to pray when we don't know how to pray.

- How often do we miss the purposes of God because we simply do not give enough time to waiting on Him?

- To worship in a tongue makes all the difference to our worship. Here the Holy Spirit gives us the words to use and they flow easily and freely like tumbling rivers of praise.

- For prayer in tongues to be edifying, it is necessary to linger longer before the Lord. As we commune with Him in loving attendance, the true depths of spiritual communion begin to be explored.

- It takes time for the human spirit to express itself fully and openly to the Lord.

- When the Spirit invades our prayers, they are transformed!

Notes

1   NRSV.
2   Although these testimonies are quoted with permission of the students concerned, all names have been changed.

Chapter 16

'Wisdom Among the Mature'
(1 Corinthians 2:6)

Prayer in the Spirit is a mark of maturity

Over the years, several 'horror stories' have been circulated about people who speak in tongues being mentally unstable.

When, as a teenager, I was first immersed in the Spirit in 1952, people warned me that I was treading on very dangerous ground. One said I was suffering from self-hypnosis. Another dismissed it as dangerous emotionalism. Others feared I had yielded to some form of demonism. I was told a fearful tale of a young lady in our city who had spoken in tongues and then, as a result, two weeks later been admitted to a mental institution, where she languished still.

Books were given to me to read which told of false claims, dishonest practice and wild ecstasy. At best, tongue-speakers were thought of as harmless cranks; at worst as dangerously deluded.

My personal difficulty was twofold. First of all, among the few hundred such people I had come across, I hadn't met any who fitted these descriptions. They all seemed normal, ordinary, godly people. They sang the same songs other Christians sang. They prayed fervently, it was true, but the prayers were Christ-centred and love-motivated in a way I had never encountered before. They loved the Bible and they were eager evangelists. If this was mental instability or demonic delusion, it was very strange, to say the least.

Secondly, I knew my own experience. I now loved Jesus more than I ever had before. I had a passion for the Scriptures. I was able to pray for hours instead of minutes. I felt more intimate with God.

I used to rise an hour or two before breakfast to pray and read the Word. On cold winter mornings, I would sit in my unheated sleepout, wrapped in scarf and overcoat, huddled over my little study table, as I meditated on God's Word. Or I would kneel by my bed, my Bible open before me as I alternately read and prayed.

I wrote a commentary on the Gospel of Mark which, no doubt, was stumbling and immature and which, mercifully, no one ever read. But I came to grips with Scripture in a new way. I pondered John's Gospel and was able to summarize its contents from memory. I spent hours in the Revelation, contemplating its mysteries. And, of course, I became very familiar with Acts and Corinthians.

If all this was dangerous emotionalism or satanic deception, I could not understand how. Being immersed in the Holy Spirit and praying in tongues had introduced me to a new level of spirituality that I never wanted to lose. I felt more stable, more spiritual, more emotionally alive, more useable to God than I ever had before. That awareness is still with me today, some fifty years later.

Nevertheless, the idea that tongue-speaking is associated with aberrant behaviour has been widespread in the literature on the subject. George Cutten, a Baptist minister and educator, set the pace in 1927 when he alleged that charismatics were people who found it hard to express themselves in normal speech, were generally of low mental ability and had little capacity for rational thought.[1] Cutten made further assumptions of psycho-pathology, hysteria and schizophrenia among tongue-speakers which were widely accepted without critical question until more recent times.

Virginia Hine recounts an interesting situation in which four psychologists were given the results of personality tests under-taken by a traditional church group and a radical tongue-speaking group. The clinicians were asked, on the basis of the results alone, to identify each group. They all assigned to the traditional group the results which showed them to be less neurotic, less distressed psychologically and less repressive. In fact, these were the results for the tongue-speakers.[2] Hine goes on to note that the psychologists had apparently assumed that the traditional group would be better adjusted and had drawn their conclusions accordingly.

Stanley Plog (1966) found no evidence of atypical personality patterns among the Pentecostal group he researched and nor did L.P. Gerlach (1966). They did note, however, that many church groups attract people who are already psychologically troubled and that this could tend to affect the results of personality tests.[3] It would seem a fair comment here that if tongue-speaking groups actually report positive results in this area, they are clearly offering genuine aid to such people.

Tongue-speaking enhances emotional stability

Interestingly, investigations have actually shown a high degree of emotional and psychological stability among glossolalists. Hummel notes that studies by the United Presbyterian Special Committee in the United States in 1970, and other research by Kildahl, McDonnell and Samarin indicate no evidence for the view that those who speak in tongues are emotionally unstable or prone to ecstatic excesses.[4] In fact, the results are quite the opposite.

Kildahl himself suggests:

> 'Almost invariably, they [i.e. tongue-speakers] said they were more cheerful, more joyful and more optimistic as a result of speaking in tongues. They were less depressed and less pessimistic and had a pervading sense of God's presence and strength within themselves ... They all seemed to report that being filled with the Spirit had made them better able to cope with frustration, and better able to show greater patience and stability in dealing with others.'[5]

In South Africa, some years ago, experiments showed that people who prayed in the Spirit were more stable, less bothered by tensions, more sensitive and displayed 'a greater ability to renounce immediate satisfactions for long-term goals'.[6]

Bittlinger also argues the beneficial side of glossolalia. He quotes Walter Hollenweger's phrase 'the psycho-hygienic function' of prayer with the spirit and then goes on to talk of the inner release of such prayer transcending the value of psycho-analysis. He quotes several psychiatric reports of tongue-speakers being positively influenced by the experience, including the South African study already mentioned.[7]

Wayne Oates, who disapproves of glossolalia, grudgingly admits that the practice does meet psychological needs such as fear, anxiety, loneliness and the like.[8]

L.M. Vivier found little difference between those who prac-tised tongue-speaking and those who did not, but he did conclude that the former were more sensitive, less bound by traditional or orthodox thought processes, less depressed, less troubled by generalized fear but more in need of emotional catharsis.[9] It would be misleading to suggest that all researchers agree with or approve of glossolalia, or that they have unveiled no problems in the lives of tongue-speakers. It also needs to be pointed out that there are significant obstacles in researching an area like this because of the nature of the subject and the difficulties in setting up valid controls. Nevertheless, there is a growing amount of clinical evidence that there is therapeutic value in praying with the spirit.

I have developed a practice in recent years of giving home-work to people who come for counsel. This varies from client to client, but it usually involves two tasks. First, I prescribe a couple of relevant passages of Scripture to learn by heart. As we have already noted, this provides the Spirit something to work on. Second, I ask them to pray with the spirit for at least fifteen minutes every day. When they have done these two things for a week, I invite them to make another appoint-ment.

It is surprising how the number of return visits from counsel-lees has diminished! There are two reasons for this. The first is that they don't do what I ask and are too ashamed to come back. And this, in a quiet way, reveals something about their willingness to work towards their own recovery. The second is that they do follow through with the reading and prayer and they don't need to come back!

Of course, further counsel is still required with some folks, even in helping them to learn how to apply the Word to their lives and how to pray with the spirit. But where people do this, wonderfully positive results can be observed.

Mature in Christ

There is an interesting statement in Paul's first letter to
the Corinthians, where he refers to one group of people as the
'mature' (1 Corinthians 2:6). The Greek word used here is *teleios*.
Literally it means 'finished', 'complete', 'perfect', 'mature' or
'whole'. In this context, it is a synonym for *pneumatikos*, which
means 'spiritual' (1 Corinthians 2:6 and 3:1).

The term is used elsewhere in the New Testament to describe
Christians who are mature in the faith. So Paul hopes the
Colossians will be *'perfect in Christ'* (Colossians 1:28) and
Epaphras prays for them to stand mature (Colossians 4:12).
James points out that perseverance helps to make us *'mature and
complete'* (1:4) and that a man who can bridle his tongue is *'a
perfect man'* (3:2). Jesus enjoins us to be *'perfect'* as our heavenly
Father is perfect (Matthew 5:48).

There also seems to be a twofold application of the word. To
the Philippians, Paul declares that he is not yet *teleios* (3:12), yet
a few verses later includes himself among those who are (3:15)!
Positionally, in Christ we are all *teleios*, but in practice we have a
long way to go!

The word also occurs in secular writings in reference to the
Greek mystery religions, where those who were initiated into
the mysteries of the cult were called *teleios*. It has been
suggested that Paul uses the word in the same way in reference
to the Corinthians who were *teleios* in regard to spiritual gifts,[10]
although there is some debate about the validity of this argument. The scholarly Delling, for example, rejects it.[11] On the
other hand, it is interesting to note that the second-century
bishop Irenaeus takes it in this sense. In his renowned *Against
Heresies*, he argued:

> 'For this reason does the apostle declare, "We speak wisdom
> among them that are perfect," terming those persons
> "perfect" who have received the Spirit of God, and who
> through the Spirit of God do speak in all languages, as he
> used himself also to speak. In like manner we do also hear
> many brethren in the Church, who possess prophetic gifts,
> and who through the Spirit speak all kinds of languages,
> and bring to light for the general benefit the hidden things

of men, and declare the "mysteries" of God, whom also the apostle terms "spiritual," they being spiritual because they partake of the Spirit...'[12]

If this is the case, it reflects the fact that just as there is maturing value in prayer and perseverance and the like, so there is in spiritual gifts, including tongue-speech. The fact that Paul alleges that he spoke in tongues more than anyone (1 Corinthians 14:18) may be relevant here, given that he was a spiritual giant.

Naturally, it would be dangerous to assume that speaking in tongues in itself makes a person mature. This is obvious from the fact that in almost the very next breath, Paul charges the Corinthians with being immature (3:1ff.)! The point is that being experienced in charismata, they **ought** to have been spiritual people. But they were not.

Maturity is clearly the result of many factors – Scripture, fellowship, baptism, communion, the pruning and purifying work of the Father and so on. But there is more than a strong suggestion here that maturity also includes praying with the spirit. And that there is corresponding benefit in such prayer. The problem with the Corinthians was not that they spoke in tongues too much; they still lagged behind Paul. The problem was that they didn't do other things enough. Glossolalia **is** a factor in spiritual maturity. But like any other, it is not enough on its own.

So to pray in the Holy Spirit includes praying with the human spirit. And when we do, we will benefit, more than we can ever know.

Don't forget

- There is therapeutic value in praying with the spirit.
- Where people learn how to apply the Word to their lives and how to pray with the Spirit, wonderfully positive results can be observed.

Notes

1 W. Mills (ed.), *Speaking in Tongues: A Guide to Research in Glossolalia* (Grand Rapids: Eerdmans, 1986), p. 442.

2 Hine in Mills (ed.), *Speaking in Tongues*, pp. 446ff.

3 W. Mills (ed.), *Speaking in Tongues*, p. 431.

4 C. Hummel, *Fire in the Fireplace* (Downers Grove: IVP, 1978), pp. 199ff.

5 J. Kildahl in Mills (ed.), *Speaking in Tongues*, pp. 364f.

6 M. Kelsey, *Tongue-Speaking: the History and Meaning of Charismatic Experience* (New York: Crossroad, 1981), pp. 204f.

7 A. Bittlinger, *Gifts and Graces* (London: Hodder and Stoughton, 1967), pp. 99ff.

8 F. Stagg, E.G. Hinson and W. Oates (eds.), *Glossolalia: Tongue Speaking in Biblical, Historical and Psychological Perspective* (Abingdon, 1967), pp. 95ff.

9 Vivier in Mills (ed.), *Speaking in Tongues*, p. 445.

10 e.g. K. Chant, *Clothed with Power* (Kingswood, NSW: Ken Chant Ministries, 1993), p. 113.

11 G. Friedrich (ed.), *Theological Dictionary of the New Testament* (Grand Rapids: Eerdmans, 1972), p. 68.

12 Irenaeus, *Against Heresies*, 5, 6, 1.

Chapter 17

'Mysteries with His Spirit...'
(1 Corinthians 14:2)

*Glossolalia is a divinely ordained form
of communication with God*

When we pray in tongues, what kind of language are we actually speaking? Is it an unlearned human tongue? Is it gibberish? Is it some kind of heavenly speech?

Human language?

Firstly, there have been many documented cases of xenolalia – of people speaking identifiable earthly languages when talking in tongues. Hard evidence is not always available as these incidents have rarely been recorded either electronically or manually. Nevertheless, there is still compelling enough anecdotal verification of genuine xenolalia.

My brother, Ken Chant, claims, 'I myself have on at least four occasions during forty years of Pentecostal ministry observed or shared in experiences where someone's glossolalia was recognized by a listener.'[1]

From personal knowledge, I know that in one of these cases a high school classics teacher recognized a glossolalic utterance as Hebrew and affirmed that Ken's interpretation was valid. Neither the speaker nor the interpreter knew any Hebrew. As a result of this, the hearer was converted to Christ.

On another occasion, a German lady affirmed that a member of Ken's church had spoken a relatively unknown provincial Prussian dialect and again that Ken's interpretation was accurate.

She was so amazed by this phenomenon she was soon filled with the Spirit herself.

Years ago, a close friend was informed that when he spoke in tongues in a church service in Adelaide, South Australia, he was using a French dialect. The late Leo Harris was once told by an astonished visitor from the Middle East that he had prayed for her in Arabic. Her son later became a minister of the gospel. On a further occasion, a Dutch pastor of my acquaintance heard a member of his congregation in a country town in Victoria speaking in German. Again, the interpretation was consistent with this. The person concerned had no knowledge of German.

Barry Silverback, an Australian missionary in Papua New Guinea, told me of an incident in a village in the Highlands where he heard someone praying in English. In Port Moresby, this would not have been unusual, but in this village it was unexpected. He was amazed to discover a man who knew no English at all, on his knees, eyes closed, saying over and over again, 'He is not in my head, He is in my heart and He has saved me.'

It has been argued that stories like these can be explained by the theory that the persons speaking were reproducing occasional foreign words or phrases that they had heard years previously but forgotten or that the utterances concerned just 'sounded like' German or Italian or whatever.[2] In the cases I have quoted, given the specific details reported, and my own knowledge of the people involved, this explanation is inadequate, to say the least.

Nevertheless, in spite of stories like these, there seem to be no biblical grounds for believing that all tongue-speaking involves known human languages. We have only one verifiable example of this in the New Testament. In every other case, it is clear that no one could comprehend what was said by the speakers. In fact, this is the normal situation – when someone speaks in tongues, *'no one understands him'* (1 Corinthians 14:2). When a human language is employed, this is possibly a combination of glossolalia and the working of miracles.

In the early days of American Pentecostalism, it was widely believed that all tongue-speaking was xenolalia. A number of would-be missionaries travelled overseas in the hope of preaching in local dialects with a gift of tongues. They all returned disappointed. They found by experience that while there may be unique occasions when human languages are spoken, these are the exception, not the norm.[3] Psychologist, John Kildahl, in fact, claims that:

> 'Of the hundreds of thousands of occasions on which glossolalia has been uttered, there is no tape recording that can be translated from a language spoken somewhere in the world ... If glossolalic utterances were somehow real languages, it would seem that there would exist somewhere in the world evidence that the speaking in tongues was in fact such a foreign language.'[4]

As we have seen, this is going too far, but, nevertheless, the general point is made that glossolalia is usually different from recognizable human speech.

Poythress argues that to validate any incident of xenolalia, controlled experimental conditions need to be in place, which is almost impossible in the circumstances. Hence, the possibility of real languages being spoken can never be either proven or disproven by normal research procedures. Unless every single case of glossolalia is investigated, the likelihood of genuine examples of xenolalia occurring is still theoretically possible.[5]

Gibberish?

Is glossolalia gibberish? Behm seems to think so when he refers to the 'babbling of glossolalia'.[7] Anderson agrees. In documenting the experiences mentioned above, he dismisses even the suggestion that the people concerned could ever have spoken real languages purely on the clearly prejudiced and plainly non-scientific basis that such a thing would be impossible.[7]

Budgen and Baxter are both convinced that glossolalia is usually the result of emotional manipulation.[8] Anthony Hoekema argues that linguists have found no resemblance between tongue-speaking and normal language and concludes that it is 'ecstatic speech'.[9] Linguist William Samarin says succinctly, 'Glossolalia is fundamentally not language'.[10]

On the other hand, others have argued that glossolalia does display recognizable language patterns. Certainly, the biblical word usually translated 'tongue' (*glossa*) means language. Had the biblical writers wanted to, they could have used an alternative term such as *battalogeo* which means to 'babble', an expression Jesus used in regard to heathen prayers (Matthew 6:7). There is no suggestion that speaking in tongues is anything other than speaking languages of some kind. William MacDonald claims: 'The Greek word *glossa* means "language" ... not mouthing nonsense syllables ... He [the tongue-speaker] has the same wholesome confidence that the one who speaks through him is the God of order. Therefore he has every reason to believe that the Spirit who speaks through him orders and shapes the speech according to intelligent patterns.'[11]

J.M. Ford agrees: '*Glossa* through the New Testament is used for human speech.'[12] Chris Kenneally, an Australian researcher, argues that discernible patterns are to be found in tongue-speech, and that these have been missed because researchers have approached the subject with preconceptions of what they are looking for.[13] They have assumed that glossolalia must of necessity contain structures similar to known languages. This is not necessarily the case.

Ken Chant shows how, if this were so, it would actually defeat the purpose of tongues:

> 'Glossolalia is the language of the spirit, why then insist that it must have a logical or coherent structure? Intelligibility, syntax, can be demanded only of that which must address its appeal to the mind. But that is the very thing glossolalia does not do! Rather, it speaks from and to the mystic spirit.
>
> Indeed, if glossolalia were subject to the laws that bind ordinary language, or if, when I speak in tongues, I must be speaking one of the native languages of men, what would I have gained? In what way would I have improved my prayer life? ... There are sentiments I could not put into words even if I were familiar with every language in the world – yet my heart yearns to sing them to God...
>
> So I do not believe that when I speak in tongues I am only speaking Swahili, or Urdu, or Chinese! If this were so, my prayer would remain bound by the limitations that inherently restrict the expressive power of all human language.

Glossolalia is free of such restraint ... But neither is it gibberish. It is rather the soaring language of the spirit.'[14]

Divine secrets

So tongue-speech is neither human language nor mumbo-jumbo. How then can we explain it? The writings of Paul may provide a useful insight when he says:

> 'For anyone who speaks in a tongue does not speak to men but to God. Indeed, no one understands him; he utters mysteries with his spirit.' (1 Corinthians 14:2)

> 'For if I pray in a tongue, my spirit prays, but my mind is unfruitful.' (1 Corinthians 14:14)

Several clear points emerge from these statements:

- Glossolalia is primarily directed towards God.
- Neither the speaker nor the hearer knows what is being said.
- The origin of tongue-speech lies in the spirit.
- When we speak in tongues, we speak 'mysteries'.
- When we speak in tongues, what we say is meaningful.

The word 'mysteries' is an interesting one. The Greek word *musterion* would be better translated 'secret'. It is used elsewhere in the New Testament to describe the hidden plan of God which was only made known through the coming of Jesus Christ (Ephesians 3:4; Colossians 1:27; 1 Timothy 3:16). So Paul tells the Corinthians that the message he preaches has been hidden for generations from the world but has now been disclosed by the Spirit (1 Corinthians 2:7ff.). In other words, a *musterion* is only a mystery because it has not been revealed.

So glossolalia is an expression of divine secrets, hidden matters known only to God and to be revealed to us when He chooses. There is no reason, then, why glossolalia should involve normal languages. The primary aim is to communicate with God, not man, deep truths known only to the Lord.

Charles Widdowson makes the intriguing suggestion that it is a form of undecodable prayer, that is, prayer which Satan does not understand and therefore cannot hinder.[15] So, when we pray in tongues, Satan is no doubt frustrated! He would love to know what we are expressing to God so that he can take action to undermine it, but he is unable to do so, for only the Spirit of God truly understands the things of God (1 Corinthians 2:11).

Furthermore, we do not know what we are praying either! So our thoughts and prejudices cannot get in the way of our prayers. This is more important than it seems at first glance. So often *we do not know what we ought to pray for* (Romans 8:26), but the Spirit does! So we are saved from foolish or selfish requests.

A thoughtful young man once said to me, 'I really can't see the point in this gibberish stuff.'

'Oh, don't call it gibberish,' I replied. 'Why not call it non-rational communication?'

'What's the difference?' he demanded, reasonably enough.

'Well,' I said. 'There are many forms of non-rational communication which are meaningful. Touch is the most obvious. In times of bereavement or grief, sometimes a touch can speak more powerfully or meaningfully than carefully chosen words could ever do. When someone is suffering grief or pain, just holding the hand or stroking the hair may be the most therapeutic thing to do. There is no intellectual content but the emotional and personal impact may be immeasurable.'

Logic is not always the best way to evaluate worth or value. As we have already seen, music is another form of non-rational communication. We may be deeply stirred by a martial song or gently moved by a romantic strain or made to feel joyful by a bright, toe-tapping melody. We may not be able to read music and we may have no idea of what instruments are being played. So there is no cognitive response, as such. But the emotional effect may be deep and lasting.

Similarly, in many ways, glossolalia has the power to affect us very deeply. It transcends rational thought, yet it is not irrational. It bypasses the powers of reason, yet it is not un-reasonable. It is a divinely ordained form of communication with God.

Like touch or music or the sweet perfume of a rose or the simple cry of a baby, it cannot be fully explained intellectually. But this does not take away from its value.

David du Plessis used to tell of a doctor who overheard a pastor speaking in tongues while he was doing his hospital visitation rounds. 'What were you saying when you were walking down the corridor yesterday?' asked the doctor. The pastor replied, 'Don't worry about that, Doctor. I was just talking to my Father in my home-town language.'

In essence, this is what glossolalia is all about.

Don't forget

- Glossolalia is primarily directed towards God.

- Glossolalia is an expression of divine secrets, hidden matters known only to God and to be revealed to us when He chooses.

- When we speak in tongues, we do not know what we are praying. So our thoughts and prejudices cannot get in the way of our prayers.

Notes

1 K. Chant, *Clothed with Power* (Kingswood, NSW: Ken Chant Ministries, 1993), p. 117.

2 W. Mills (ed.), *Speaking in Tongues: A Guide to Research in Glossolalia* (Grand Rapids: Eerdmans, 1986), p. 475.

3 R. Anderson, *Vision of the Disinherited* (New York: Oxford, 1979), p. 19.

4 Kildahl in Mills (ed.), *Speaking in Tongues*, p. 363.

5 Poythress in Mills (ed.), *Speaking in Tongues*, p. 476.

6 J. Behm, 'Parakaleo' in G. Friedrich (ed.), *Theological Dictionary of the New Testament* (Grand Rapids: Eerdmans, 1968), p. 813.

7 Anderson, *Vision of the Disinherited*, p. 19.

8 V. Budgen, *The Charismatics and the Word of God* (Welwyn: Evangelical Press, 1986), p. 71.

9 ibid., p. 71.

10 Samarin in Mills (ed.), *Speaking in Tongues*, p. 388.

11 W. MacDonald in Mills (ed.), *Speaking in Tongues*, p. 225.

12 J. Ford, in Mills (ed.), *Speaking in Tongues*, p. 277.

13 C. Kenneally, *Other Tongues*, unpublished thesis (University of Melbourne, 1990).

14 K. Chant, *Clothed with Power*, pp. 117f.

15 *New Day* (Unley Park: Tabor Publications, June 1982), p. 23.

Chapter 18

'Hear What the Spirit Says...'
(1 Corinthians 2:10)

Prayer in the Spirit means listening, too

Praying in the Holy Spirit is not just talking. It means listening, too.

This is a dimension of prayer that is often neglected. It is only too easy to consume all our time in communion with God with speech. For most believers, spoken invocations have been the norm for all of our lives. We 'say' grace before meals; we 'say' our prayers before we sleep; we 'say' the benediction at the end of a service. It is helpful to remember Jesus' warning that the heathen think the number of words they say will impress their gods (Matthew 6:7). Learning to be silent before the Lord is equally important.

Often, it takes a conscious effort to be quiet and listen to God. There are so many distractions. Modern life militates against us being still. We can even feel guilty if we are not talking or moving or doing or singing or something.

But the Scripture reminds us of our need to stop and listen to God:

> 'Be still, and know that I am God;
>   I will be exalted among the nations,
>   I will be exalted in the earth.'   (Psalm 46:10)

> 'But the LORD is in his holy temple;
>   let all the earth be silent before him.'   (Habakkuk 2:20)

'This is what the Sovereign Lord, the Holy One of Israel, says:

"In repentance and rest is your salvation, ·
in quietness and trust is your strength."'

(Isaiah 30:15)

We need to learn how to be still before God. There is, of course, a time for shouting or singing or crying out to the Lord. In fact, a quick glance at a concordance will make it plain that there are over twenty times more references to raising our voices to the Lord than there are to being quiet.[1] But there are times when we do need to close our mouths, bow our heads and humble ourselves in silent adoration and obeisance.

It is also important for us to listen to what God has to say to us. *'If my people would but listen to me,'* God said, *'if Israel would follow my ways, how quickly would I subdue their enemies and turn my hand against their foes!'* (Psalm 81:13–14). Time and again, the prophets called on people to listen. Through Isaiah, for example, God said over and over, *'Listen, O Jacob, my servant!'* (Isaiah 44:1; 46:3; 46:12; 48:1, 12, 14, 16; 49:1). The prophets Joel (1:2), Micah (1:2; 3:1; 6:1) and Zechariah (3:8) all spoke in similar terms.

Jesus often preceded His teaching with words like, 'Listen to this', or, 'Listen carefully' (e.g. Matthew 15:10; Mark 4:3; Luke 9:44). And on the Mount of Transfiguration, God's voice was heard saying, *'This is my Son, whom I love ... Listen to him!'* (Matthew 17:5).

Into all truth

Because the sons of God are led by the Spirit of God (Romans 8:14), the Holy Spirit teaches us how to recognize God's voice. It is the Spirit's role to lead us into truth so we hear what God is saying. Jesus taught this very plainly:

'But when he, the Spirit of truth, comes, he will guide you into all truth. He will not speak on his own; he will speak only what he hears, and he will tell you what is yet to come. He will bring glory to me by taking from what is mine and making it known to you.'   (John 16:13–14)

There are three major points being made here:

- Firstly, the Spirit is the Spirit of truth. So if we desire to avoid error, we must learn to hear what He says to us.
- Secondly, the Counsellor Himself hears from the Father. In the same way, we must learn how to hear from Him.
- Thirdly, the Spirit brings Jesus to us in a meaningful way.

It is crucial to pray in the Spirit – but to listen while we do! Seven times in the book of Revelation, we read these words: *'He who has an ear, let him hear what the Spirit says to the churches'* (Revelation 2:7, 11, 17, 29; 3:6, 13, 22).

Words could not be plainer. If we are to please God we must listen to what He says. There are many biblical commands to listen to God's Word. If we are to obey Him, we must know His commands. If we are to follow Him, we must know where He is going. If we are to preach His Word, we must know what He is saying.

As we have already noted, the Spirit's words to us will always be consistent with Scripture. It is inconceivable that it could be otherwise. In fact, more often than not, He will speak to us **through** the Scripture. But we also need to remember that in the early Church, there was no New Testament. Those first-century disciples were almost totally dependent on their awareness of the Spirit's voice. To tell the truth, in practical terms, we are sometimes not much better off. Although we have Bibles, we do not know them as well as we ought. We are abysmally ignorant of huge slabs of Scripture. In real terms, we may actually know less than some of the believers of biblical times. At least they usually had access to the Old Testament. Many early congregations had a gospel or two or a handful of epistles (cf. Colossians 4:16). If they knew these very well, as indeed they might, their total **working knowledge** of the New Testament may have been greater than ours!

Some years ago, on an overseas trip, I discovered to my dismay that I had inadvertently left my Bible at home. As an exercise on the plane, I decided to write out scriptures from memory. I was pleased with how much I did know of a few passages. But I was dismayed and alarmed at how little I could reproduce of the rest. It's an interesting experiment to undertake.

Given our general ignorance of the Bible, we still need desperately to hear what the Spirit is saying to us. Praying in the Spirit means listening closely for His voice. Not to add to the written word of God – it is never allowable to do this – but to direct our attention to it.

Paul details this ministry clearly in his letter to the Corinthians. It is the Spirit's role, he teaches, to reveal to us the things which God has prepared for those who love Him (1 Corinthians 2:9). How does He do this?

The deep things of God

First of all, the Spirit Himself searches out *'the deep things of God'* (1 Corinthians 2:10). What He first discovers, He then discloses. The point is that it is only the Spirit who can do this. Just as only the human spirit knows the human heart, so only the Holy Spirit knows the heart of God. This is a powerful analogy. No matter how well we think we know one another, there are depths we can never explore. Only we ourselves know all that lies deep within us. Similarly, we can never know the hidden thoughts of God unless He chooses to reveal them – and He only does that by His Spirit.

So *'no eye has seen, no ear has heard, no mind has conceived what God has prepared'* (1 Corinthians 2:9). Paul makes the same point very strongly elsewhere:

> *'Oh, the depth of the riches of the wisdom and knowledge*
>   *of God!*
>   *How unsearchable his judgments,*
>   *and his paths beyond tracing out!*
>   *Who has known the mind of the Lord?*
>   *Or who has been his counsellor?*
>   *Who has ever given to God,*
>   *that God should repay him?*
>   *For from him and through him and to him are all things.*
>   *To him be the glory for ever! Amen.'*
>   (Romans 11:33–36)

In human terms, the answer to these questions is, 'No one.' But in divine terms, the answer is, 'The Holy Spirit.' He does know the mind of God and He is acquainted with His purposes, for He is the Spirit of God. This does not necessarily mean, of course, that He will tell us all He knows. It is God's divine prerogative to withhold knowledge from us if He so chooses. But if anyone is going to make such knowledge known, it can only be the Holy Spirit.

So Paul explains that the gospel he preaches has been taught to him by the Holy Spirit (1 Corinthians 2:13). This is, of course, a clear fulfilment of the promise of Jesus that the Counsellor would lead the disciples into truth and remind them of the things He had taught (John 14:25; 16:13).

Furthermore, those who have received the Spirit of God now understand the charismata, the free gifts of God. The verb implies 'to know without doubt'. There are many wonderful gifts we could mention here. The greatest of God's gifts is salvation. So the Spirit enables us to comprehend a little of the wonder of grace that made this possible. In particular, He continues to reveal Christ to us, enabling us to confess Him as Saviour and Lord (1 Corinthians 12:3).

The Bible is another gift from God. This is one of the compelling reasons why Christians regard the Bible as the written Word of God. The Spirit who inspired it also affirms its authenticity to our hearts. We know it is from the Lord.

There is also a clear reference here to spiritual gifts. When the Holy Spirit comes into our hearts, He identifies and confirms the genuineness of spiritual graces. We know that these, too, are genuine, for the Spirit bears witness that it is so.

Furthermore, we are able to combine spiritual matters cohesively (1 Corinthians 2:13). We bring them together in a godly way, balancing them for the good of all (cf. 1 Corinthians 12:7). As one of the Greek words used here can be seen as either masculine or neuter, some translators render this passage *'interpreting spiritual things to those who are spiritual'* (NRSV). In other words, spiritual people are able to interpret spiritual matters correctly. Clearly, this, too, implies sensitivity to the Spirit for it is only spiritual people who can hear the Spirit's voice:

> *'The man without the Spirit does not accept the things that come from the Spirit of God, for they are foolishness to him, and he*

cannot understand them, because they are spiritually discerned. The spiritual man makes judgments about all things, but he himself is not subject to any man's judgment.'

(1 Corinthians 2:14–15)

Paul uses two contrasting terms in this passage. The first is *psuchikos* which basically means 'soulish' and which has been imported into English in words like 'psychology' and 'psychoanalysis'. In the New Testament it is always used disparagingly with connotations of being unspiritual or even carnal (e.g. James 3:15). Among some Greek philosophers, the word was used in a noble sense, to distinguish those who concentrated on matters of the soul and mind rather than those of the physical body.[2] Even so, says Paul, the *psuchikos* person still cannot apprehend the things of God. Such a one may represent unregenerate nature at its best, but it is still insufficient for the task. More than reason and philosophy is needed. It is, as one commentator puts it, like deaf men judging music.[3]

So we have the second word *pneumatikos* which means 'spiritual'. It is the spiritual person who hears the voice of the Spirit and discerns spiritual truth. A *pneumatikos* is one who demonstrates both the gifts (1 Corinthians 12:1; 14:1) and the fruit of the Spirit (Galatians 6:1). Obviously, this involves being filled with the Spirit and walking in the Spirit.

Clearly, while the *psuche*, the soul, is not unimportant – Jesus tells us to love the Lord with all our soul (Mark 12:30) – we still need the help of the Holy Spirit to perceive **spiritual** realities. Obviously, then, it is vitally important, to yield our lives to God's Spirit and submit daily to Him.

Praying in the Spirit means allowing the Spirit to do His vital task of bringing Christ to us and guiding our lives into all truth. If we do not listen, we frustrate the Spirit's task.

Listen to the Lord

The prophet Habakkuk provides a helpful model of one who learned how to listen to the Lord. The first chapter is easy to identify with. The prophet talks virtually non-stop to God. He is so much like us. But then he begins the second by declaring,

> '*I will stand at my watch*
>   *and station myself on the ramparts;*
> *I will look to see what he will say to me . . . '*

(Habakkuk 2:1)

It is important to reach the point where we are not only willing to hear what the Lord will say, but are actually determined to station ourselves before Him until He does speak.

Not that we can force God to talk to us, of course. But if we never stay quiet we will never hear what He has to say. The medieval mystics learned great secrets here. They developed the contemplative life to a fine art. People like Thomas à Kempis, Teresa of Avila and Mother Julian of Norwich knew much of the power of stillness in God's presence. In 1427, the gentle Thomas, for instance, wrote:

> 'Seek a convenient time to retire into thyself and meditate often upon God's loving-kindnesses ... The greatest saints avoided the society of men, when they could conveniently, and did rather choose to serve God, in secret . . . ' [4]

In 1373, the thirty-year-old Julian, a young recluse at St Julian's Church, Norwich, and the first English woman known to have written a book, said these words:

> 'To focus on the goodness of God is the highest form of prayer, and God's goodness comes down to meet us at our most basic needs ... It is God's will that we see Him and search for Him; it is His will that we wait for Him and trust Him.' [5]

Waiting on the Lord is a vital part of what it means to pray in the Holy Spirit. And this means taking time with God. There's no other alternative.

Don't forget

- Praying in the Holy Spirit is not just talking. It means listening, too.

- We need to learn how to be still before God.

- There is a time for shouting or singing or crying out to the Lord. But there are times when we do need to close our mouths, bow our heads and humble ourselves in silent adoration and obeisance.

- Words could not be plainer. If we are to please God we must listen to what He says.

- The Spirit's words to us will always be consistent with Scripture. In fact, more often than not, He will speak to us **through** the Scripture.

- We need the help of the Holy Spirit to perceive **spiritual** realities.

- Praying in the Spirit means allowing the Spirit to do His vital task of bringing Christ to us and guiding our lives into all truth. If we do not listen, we frustrate the Spirit's task.

Notes

1   In the New International Version of the Bible, although there are less than ten references to being silent or quiet before the Lord, there are over fifty to the words of our mouths, shouting and the like, around fifty to trumpet calls and the sound of musical instruments and well over one hundred to singing.

2   G.G. Findlay, *St Paul's First Epistle to the Corinthians* in *The Expositor's Greek Testament* Volume II (Grand Rapids: Eerdmans, 1967), p. 783.

3   ibid., p. 784.

4   1980, pp. 60f.

5   Julian of Norwich, *Revelations of Divine Love* (London: Hodder and Stoughton, 1987), pp. 12, 21.

Chapter 19

'The Eyes of Your Heart Enlightened...'
(Ephesians 1:18)

We need a spirit of wisdom and revelation

In order to hear the voice of God we need to learn how to listen.

Sometimes He does speak in the hurly-burly of life. But often it is not in the wind or the earthquake or the fire. Usually, when all the fury is past, and there is *'sheer silence'* (1 Kings 19:12 NRSV), then the 'still, small voice' of the Lord is heard.

I remember struggling as a young Christian to identify the Spirit's voice. Of all the sounds clamouring for my attention, I strove to recognize which one was His. I anguished over that. And my anguish drove me to my knees. There, in my desperation, I learned to recognize the one voice I needed to hear.

I discovered the old principle that the best way to get to know God's will was to get to know God. So I began to seek God Himself. The result was, of course, that I began more readily to understand His will. There is no substitute for time spent waiting on God. Jesus said, *'My sheep listen to my voice'* (John 10:27). As we pray in the Spirit, this becomes more and more true.

There are practical things we can do, of course, like removing outer distractions and finding, as Jesus often did, a lonely place to pray (Mark 1:35; Luke 5:16; 6:12; 9:28). It is well known how Susanna Wesley simply threw her apron over her head and her many children knew that she was in her 'prayer closet' (cf. Matthew 6:6).

It is wise to find an appropriate posture that doesn't lead to cramp or sleep and to quieten the mind, by putting urgent matters to one side, perhaps by writing them down so you can attend to them later.

God's word is spontaneous

How do we recognize God's voice? Mark Virkler suggests:

> 'This is the voice of God: a chance idea that intersects your mind, not flowing from the normal, meditative process, but simply appearing in your heart'.[1]

In other words, when God speaks, it is usually spontaneous and instantaneous. It just 'drops into your mind'. God's voice is a flow of spontaneous thoughts. He uses our normal thought processes as a vehicle, especially the imagination. Just as temptation results from a thought being conceived in the heart and then developing until it results in action (James 1:14f.), so does a leading from God. There's nothing mystical or magical about it. But when a thought comes from the Lord, there is a specialness about it, too. There are several identifiable characteristics of a word from God:

- It is usually light and gentle (1 Kings 19:12).
- It is accompanied by a sense of peace (Philippians 4:7; Colossians 3:15).
- It is accompanied by a sense of assurance (Romans 8:16f.; 1 John 5:14f.).
- It may have unusual content – it can be at variance with our own thoughts (Isaiah 55:8f.).
- It usually has greater depth and insight than our own thoughts (Isaiah 55:8f.; Romans 11:34).
- It usually produces a special reaction within us such as excitement, conviction, peace, faith or awe (Genesis 32:30; Acts 9:5ff.; Revelation 1:17).[2]
- It brings with it the strength to perform whatever is required (Daniel 10:19).
- It is persistent, even in the face of contrary evidence (cf. 2 Kings 2:1ff.; Acts 20:23; 21:13f.).

There are, no doubt, other qualities of the voice of the Lord. In the ultimate, we each have to learn for ourselves to recognize the sound when we hear it. It is almost certain He addresses each of us differently. To hear and identify the way He speaks takes time, patience and experience – and waiting on God!

There is an old tale of a farmer who visited the city. In the bustling, noisy street, he stopped his friend and said, 'Listen!'

'I don't hear anything,' his friend replied.

'I heard a bird singing,' said the farmer.

A few paces further along, the friend stopped. Grabbing the farmer's arm, he said, 'Did you hear that?'

'What?' replied the puzzled farmer.

'Someone dropped some money!' said the friend.

We hear what we are attuned to hear. God wants us to be attuned to Him.

The goal is not a total blanking of the mind, as in Eastern meditation, but a refocusing of our thoughts and attention. Mark Virkler wisely writes:

> 'The goal in achieving inner stillness is to **know** deep within ourselves the movement of God ... It is being in touch with the Lord Jesus Christ within.'[3]

In fact, when we focus on Christ, we see more clearly! Paul prays that we may have a *'spirit of wisdom and revelation'* and that *'the eyes of our hearts may be enlightened'* (Ephesians 1:17–18).

There are four major results of this:

- that we may know Him better
- that we may know the hope to which He has called us
- that we may know the riches of His glorious inheritance in the saints
- that we may know His incomparably great power for us who believe.

Each of these has enormous promise and potential in our lives. As we pray, and the Spirit teaches us, we are introduced to great blessings.

Spiritual insight

The capacity to 'see' with the 'eyes of the heart' is a spiritual one. It is particularly linked with the fullness of the Spirit. The prophet Joel promised that 'visions and dreams' would result from the outpouring of the Holy Spirit (Joel 2:28), a promise repeated by Peter on the Day of Pentecost (Acts 2:17ff.). David prayed,

> 'Open my eyes that I may see
> wonderful things in your law.'   (Psalm 119:18)

Such spiritual vision has always been the language of the Holy Spirit. 'When a prophet of the LORD is among you,' God said to Aaron and Miriam, 'I reveal myself to him in visions, I speak to him in dreams' (Numbers 12:6). Centuries later, the prophet Hosea made a similar statement (Hosea 12:10). Habakkuk said, 'I will look to see what he will say to me' (Habakkuk 2:1). This is why prophets were often called 'seers' (1 Chronicles 29:29; Amos 7:12). They could, to paraphrase Wordsworth, 'see into the life of things'.

Such prophetic vision is still part of the Spirit-filled life. God's Holy Spirit often shows us His truth visually. A friend of mine claims He does this because He knows we like picture books better than textbooks!

So it is not unusual when we pray to see mental images, visual pictures, imaginative scenes through which God's Spirit teaches us. This is why it is so important to linger with God in prayer. When we do, the Spirit can show us many wonderful revelations.

Dreams and visions

These may occur as literal dreams (Acts 16:9). Often, they will be what we might call 'waking pictures'. Twice, in the New Testament, the word 'trance' is used to describe this (Acts 10:10–16; 11:5; 22:17). We need to understand that this does not mean a hypnotic condition or a state of ecstasy, as it commonly does today. The Greek word *ekstasis* means 'a state of wonder or amazement'. Its literal meaning is 'standing outside oneself'. It is used rather in the way we would talk about a person being 'beside himself' with joy. The noun, or its accompanying verb, is employed, for instance, to describe the amazement of the crowds when they saw Jesus healing a blind man (Matthew 12:23) or raising a paralytic (Mark 2:12) or calming a storm (Mark 6:51). Similarly, the women at the tomb were in a state of *ekstasis* (Mark 16:8), and the crowds at Pentecost (Acts 2:7, 12) and the believers at the conversion of Saul (Acts 9:21) were 'amazed'.

So to be in a trance as Peter was when he saw the vision that led him to the house of Cornelius (Acts 10:10; 11:5) or like Paul when God told him to leave Jerusalem (Acts 22:17), was simply to be in a condition of heightened awareness and awe of the Spirit of God.

Usually, visions like this come unexpectedly. This seems to have been the case with Ananias (Acts 9:10–11). Very often, however, it is when we are praying that God reveals Himself, as He did with Peter (Acts 10:9).

Is it right to ask God for such visions? This question is better phrased, 'Is it right to ask God to reveal His purpose?' When we put it like this, we leave the method of revelation up to God. Nevertheless, by using our imagination to picture a situation which may be the focus of our prayers, we can increase our sensitivity to God in this area. In normal practice, it seems that a vision comes spontaneously and without warning. It flashes onto the screen of the mind in a moment. Suddenly, it is there. There is probably a reason for this. The Spirit needs to get in quickly, before, like fiddling technicians, we adjust and distort the image.

In 1978, I was in the midst of a time of earnestly seeking God for my future. I had been praying for months, without any real clarity. There had been indicators of God's purpose, but I was finding them difficult to comprehend. At that time, I visited Sweden for two weeks of ministry. The first morning there I woke up and it was as if I was watching television. There before me was a short documentary, as it were, of a teaching centre called 'Tabor' which I was to establish in Australia. I knew it was a picture from God. Suddenly all the other indications I had received fell into place and made sense. There was no doubt, now. This was from the Lord.

I became so excited, I hopped out of bed and wrote it all down in my travel dairy. Then I became over-enthusiastic and added a few ideas of my own. Later, I had to scratch these out again! It was just as well the Spirit took hold of my imagination first.

Subsequently, I shared the details of the vision with others and ultimately they also agreed it was from God. Today, many years later, it has become a reality.

I don't usually have visions as dramatic as that. But I do often 'see' things in the spirit. For me, as in Sweden, this is frequently first thing in the morning, even before I rise. It seems my mind is uncluttered then and God's Spirit has most chance of getting through!

One further point. As I did with my travel diary, it is often helpful to jot things down that the Lord shows us, if only to be able to reflect on them later, when they have been fulfilled. The Lord commanded Habakkuk to do this (Habakkuk 2:2). And, of course, many of the prophets did likewise, as their books bear eloquent testimony.

We are not trying to write another Bible! Not everything that biblical heroes wrote has been preserved in Scripture (1 Chronicles 28:19; 29:29; 1 Kings 4:32). But there is value in recording what God says to us, if only to make sure we don't forget.

Word and church

Naturally, as I have stressed elsewhere, the Spirit will never give us a revelation which contravenes Scripture. No matter how convincing a vision may seem to be, if it is not biblical it is to be rejected without question (Deuteronomy 13:1–4). Everything we need to know about God has been made known to us in Christ (Hebrews 1:1–4). Whatever the Lord shows us in prayer will always be consistent with this. It will never add to it. It will only ever help us to live more fully in the light of the revelation already given us in the written Word.

So the Spirit may well show us things about ourselves, our church, or our family, or the world. He may direct us to certain lines of action or behaviour. But they will only involve implementation of what is already in the Bible, never anything additional to it.

Secondly, whatever revelation we receive must always be confirmed by fellow believers. If others do not bear witness to it, it must be examined very carefully and possibly even rejected. 'In the mouth of two or three witnesses, let every word be established', is a sound and oft-repeated biblical principle (Deuteronomy 17:6; 19:15; Matthew 18:16; 2 Corinthians 13:1; 1 Timothy 5:19; Hebrews 10:28). This is why prophetic utterances are to be examined for veracity (1 Corinthians 14:29; 1 Thessalonians 5:19–21). It also provides one of the many reasons why we need to be part of a local body of believers. Otherwise, where can we turn for reassurance and protection? So the church provides a second point of reference for the validity of our experience.

Thirdly, we need to have a humble, teachable spirit. If we become arrogant or self-righteous about the fact that God has spoken to us, we betray the very nature of His word. Prayer in the Spirit is always in harmony with the fruit of the Spirit (Galatians 5:23). The moment we boast about a word from God, we invalidate it.

But when we pray in the Spirit, and He does speak to us, the result can be powerful and encouraging. Praying in the Spirit, then, means both hearing and seeing the things the Lord shows us. When we keep both the ears and the eyes of our hearts open when we pray, we can far more easily draw near to God. When we do, we have His assurance, that He will, in turn, draw near to us (James 4:8).

Don't forget

- The best way to get to know God's will is to get to know God.
- When God speaks, it is usually spontaneous and instantaneous.
- Spiritual vision has always been the language of the Holy Spirit.
- Is it right to ask God for visions? This question is better phrased, 'Is it right to ask God to reveal His purpose?' When we put it like this, we leave the method of revelation up to God.

- The Spirit will never give us a revelation which contravenes Scripture.
- Whatever revelation we receive must always be confirmed by fellow believers.
- We need to have a humble, teachable spirit. If we become arrogant or self-righteous about the fact that God has spoken to us, we betray the very nature of His word.

Notes

1   Mark Virkler, *Dialogue with God* (Peacemakers, 1987), p. 28.

2   G. Fitzpatrick, *How to Recognize God's Voice* (Tonbridge: Sovereign World, 2001).

3   Virkler, *Dialogue with God*, p. 44.

Chapter 20

'Today ... Do Not Harden Your Hearts'

(Hebrews 3:7)

Prayer in the Spirit means being filled with the Spirit

As we have seen, praying in the Spirit includes all kinds of prayer, both in our own language and the language of the Spirit.

New birth

How do we pray in the Spirit? Clearly, the first step is to be born again. Jesus taught plainly that if we are not born again, we cannot even see the kingdom of God (John 3:3–5). New birth is a work of the Spirit – it is He who infuses new life into us. Again, Jesus made this very clear:

> *'I tell you the truth, no one can enter the kingdom of God unless he is born of water and the Spirit. Flesh gives birth to flesh, but the Spirit gives birth to spirit.'* (John 3:5–6)

The meaning is plain. Unless the Spirit regenerates us, we are shut off from the kingdom.

The Greek word for 'again' can also mean 'from above'. New birth is a heavenly birth, brought about by God's Spirit. What happens is that He Himself dwells within us and our spirits becomes one with His. So Paul writes,

> *'He who unites himself with the Lord is one with him in spirit.'* (1 Corinthians 6:17)

Again, it is the Holy Spirit who bears witness with our spirits that we are the children of God (Romans 8:17). Indeed, if the Spirit of Christ is not in us, we do not belong to Him (Romans 8:9).

The Holy Spirit begins the process of new birth by convicting us of our sin (John 16:8). Unless we recognize our need of Christ and believe that He died for our sins, we cannot be born again.

Filled with the Spirit

Obviously, to pray in the Spirit means to have the Spirit in us. Otherwise it is clearly impossible. This does not necessarily mean being filled with the Spirit. Being Spirit-filled is not automatic. It doesn't just happen. The fact that it is a biblical command, makes it clear that there is responsibility on our part (Ephesians 5:18).

The New Testament is quite clear on how the Spirit comes into our lives. Unhappily, there has been a great deal of debate about this and much confusion. Part of the problem is that we have tried to make theological definitions out of free-flowing biblical metaphors.

Metaphors

The term 'baptize' in the Spirit is a metaphor. It basically means to 'immerse'. It is used interchangeably with other similar metaphors – fill, fall on, gift, seal, receive, pour out and so on (Acts 2:4, 17, 38; 10:44ff.; 11:15–17; 19:2). Because these **are** metaphors, we need to avoid locking them in too closely with fixed meanings. Biblical metaphors are often used differently in different contexts. For instance, a lion is used both as a metaphor for the Lord Jesus Christ (Revelation 5:5) and the devil (1 Peter 5:8)! Yeast is used as an example of both the growth of the kingdom of God (Matthew 13:33) and also of sinister, pervasive sin (Matthew 16:6, 11; cf. 1 Corinthians 5:6–8). So Paul may be using the phrase 'immerse in the Spirit' (1 Corinthians 12:13) in a different way from the Synoptics (Matthew 3:11; Luke 3:16; Acts 1:5).

In the light of this, we should avoid making the term a shibboleth. Much harm has been done to the cause of Christ by arguing about definition. The ministry of the Spirit in our lives is a matter for discipleship, not debate!

It is also interesting that only the verb ('baptize') is used in the New Testament in regard to the Spirit. The noun ('baptism') does not occur in this context. This also implies an emphasis on experiencing the blessing rather than debating the doctrine. Theological labels are much more a modern phenomenon than a biblical one.

Potentially ours

It is important to realize that both the person and the power of the Holy Spirit are potentially ours. Paul makes this sky-blue clear in his letter to the Ephesians. The first chapter is crammed with positive affirmations about this. First of all, he declares that all the blessings of God have already been made available to us in Christ (1:3ff.). Blessing, adoption, redemption, forgiveness, grace, election, authority, new life, victory – all these have been given to us in Christ. There is nothing more that God can do for us. We are complete in Christ (Colossians 2:9, 10). All the treasures of wisdom and knowledge are found in Him (Colossians 2:3). All things are ours in Him (1 Corinthians 3:21ff.). This includes the Holy Spirit.

Experience shows, however, that many Christians are not enjoying all these blessings. Either they are not aware of them or they are not willing to have them or they do not claim them. Michael Green comments, 'It is no use making out an extensive list of the treasures in our inheritance if we do not make use of them.'[1] In the light of this, many believers are potentially filled with the Holy Spirit, but not actually so.

A discrete experience

A study of Acts makes it obvious that it is possible to believe and not be filled with the Holy Spirit. It is sometimes argued that doctrine should not be drawn from Acts, but in the case of the initial reception of the Spirit, there is no other book which offers us specific documentary evidence. And given that the experiences of the Spirit recorded in Acts all stem from divine initiative, not from human action, it is appropriate to accept them as models for the whole church age. Furthermore, there are significant biblical precedents for applying lessons drawn from narrative passages to our lives today (John 3:14–15; 1 Corinthians 10:11; Hebrews 1:1ff.).

Acts chapters 8 and 19, in particular, demonstrate clear-cut cases of people who were plainly converted to Christ and later baptized in the Spirit. As far as the Samaritans are concerned, there is no doubt about it. At the very least, some days elapsed between their dramatic conversion to Christ and the outpouring of the Spirit. At Ephesus, Paul's opening question, *'Did you receive the Holy Spirit when you believed?'* (Acts 19:2) is particularly pertinent, as it clearly implies the possibility of being a disciple of Christ without having received the Spirit. If this were not so, there is no point to the question.

Various interpretations have been placed on these events – that they were related to the establishment of the kingdom in different ethnic groups, or that they were necessary because of the absence of a written Word and so on. None of these is particularly convincing. The fact is that, however we explain them, they still demonstrate the possibility of being a believer without being immersed in the Spirit. The latter is an experience discrete from conversion.

Even in the life of Jesus, we see the same distinction. In terms of His earthly life, from the moment of His conception by the Holy Spirit, He was the Son of God (Luke 1:35). Yet thirty years later, the Holy Spirit came 'upon' Him (Luke 3:21–22). It was only after this that He worked any signs, wonders or miracles. He was eternally the Son, clearly indwelt by the Spirit, yet He still experienced a subsequent empowering.

'In' or 'on'?

This distinction between being indwelt by the Spirit and immersed in the Spirit is further indicated by the use of two small prepositions, *en* ('in') and *epi* ('upon'). While prepositions are often employed fairly loosely in the Greek New Testament, in this context these two are used consistently. In many places, the Spirit is said to be 'in' (*en*) us (Romans 8:9; 1 Corinthians 6:19, 20; 2 Corinthians 13:14; Galatians 2:20; Colossians 1:27). In other cases, He is said to come 'upon' (*epi*) us (Luke 24:49;

Acts 1:8; 2:17; 8:16; 10:44, 45; 19:6). At first glance, this may seem like a play on words, but the distinction is plain. The point is that it is possible to have the Holy Spirit 'in' us without having Him come 'upon' us.

The Spirit indwells us to give us life – He comes upon us to empower us for greater effectiveness in service.

Taking a clue from the Greek word *energema*, which is used in the New Testament in reference to the power of the Spirit (e.g. 1 Corinthians 12:10), it is possible to draw a useful analogy with heat energy. Every one of us needs heat 'within' us to stay alive. Throw us into the North Sea and, like the passengers from the ill-fated *Titanic*, we will die within minutes. In normal circumstances, however, by the use of warm clothing and heating appliances, we also apply heat energy 'upon' us for greater comfort, efficiency, and well-being. We are alive anyway, and will hopefully stay that way, but the additional energy enables us to function more effectively.

Similarly, it is possible to be a Christian believer, truly regenerate, truly justified and sanctified and truly indwelt by the Holy Spirit, and yet still not empowered by the Spirit. It is the same Holy Spirit, of course, but a different way of working.

A seal

In both 2 Corinthians 1:21ff. and Ephesians 1:13, the Holy Spirit is described as a 'seal'. In biblical times, a seal was used to identify ownership and to express authentication and security. It was not necessarily strong. Often it was just an imprint on wax. But it was obvious when it was violated, as it could not be restored. Documents were often sealed in this way for privacy (Revelation 5:1). Pilate put a seal on the tomb of Jesus as a mark of his authority (Matthew 27:66). In the same way, the Holy Spirit seals, that is, authenticates and secures our salvation. He is a 'guarantee' of our ultimate redemption (2 Corinthians 1:21f.).[2]

A seal is not the same as the matter it seals – nor is its application necessarily contemporaneous with it. Ephesians 1:13 makes this apparent. The action of believing clearly precedes that of being sealed with the Spirit.[3] In fact, Paul is reminding his readers of the birth of their church, where the first members were 'sealed' with the Holy Spirit after they believed and were baptized in water (Acts 19:1–7).

Common factors

Significantly, in the five records we have in Acts of people being immersed in the Spirit (Acts 2:1–4; 8:1–25; 9:17; 10:1–48; 19:1–7), there are some indisputable common factors. They can be summarized simply. Whenever there was an outpouring of the Spirit, it was:

- immediate (sudden)
- powerful (supernatural)
- distinctive (singular)
- observable (seen).

In every case, the Spirit comes suddenly. There is no New Testament record of any believer receiving the Spirit gradually. (He 'falls' on them; He is 'poured out' – He does not 'dribble' on them or 'seep' into them!) He always comes powerfully. Something happens when the Spirit falls. There is a power encounter. His coming is always distinctive – it is not only marked by more general evidences of joy, love, peace and delight, but by evidences which are undeniably and uniquely signs that it is the Holy Spirit who has come. He always comes observably. In every case, not only do those who are baptized in the Spirit know it has happened, but other witnesses also know. (This latter point is significant because it makes it plain that when people were immersed it could not have been either secret or gradual.)

An immediate sign

Finally, in every case, speaking in tongues is either clearly mentioned or implied as the normal, initial evidence of the reception of the Spirit. Indeed, when the Jewish believers with Peter heard Romans praying in tongues, they immediately recognized that this was a sign that the Spirit had come upon them (Acts 10:46). As for the reluctant Peter, *'Who was I,'* he asks, *'to think that I could oppose God?'* (Acts 11:17).

The Ephesus story also confirms that glossolalia was the accepted immediate sign of Spirit-baptism. The record contains an intriguing, apparently insignificant, grammatical construction which is more weighty than appears at first glance. In the sentence, *'the Holy Spirit came on them, and they spoke in tongues and prophesied'* (Acts 19:6), the usual and very common word for 'and' (*kai*) does not occur. Instead, Luke uses the relatively rare enclitic particle *te*, which implies a causal connection between the two clauses. It can be roughly translated 'and so'. The Holy Spirit came on them 'and so' they spoke in tongues. This construction suggests that in Luke's mind, at least, the one would naturally follow the other. It is probably fair to conclude that Luke's contemporaries felt the same way.

To summarize, the pattern of the Acts of the Apostles is that experiencing the fullness of the Spirit is distinct from conversion and that it is an experience usually identified by glossolalia.

To pray in the Spirit, we need to be filled with the Spirit. When the Spirit invades our lives, He also invades our prayers! So we need to invite Him into our prayer life that it might be truly impregnated by the living presence of God! In New Testament terms, this means asking God to immerse us in the Spirit and then by faith exercising the prayer-gift of glossolalia.

Yielding to the Spirit

Being immersed in the Spirit involves an ongoing relationship with the Holy Spirit. It means walking in the Spirit and being led by the Spirit. Above all, it means yielding to the Spirit. Sadly, it is possible to begin well in the Spirit but not to continue. This was the problem faced by the Galatians (Galatians 3:3). They had started in the Spirit but were ending in the flesh. They had reverted to legalism, obeying the dictates of law instead of the voice of the Spirit.

This is why some people speak in tongues but show little other evidence of a Spirit-filled life. They are still paddling in the shadows of their entrance into the spiritual realm. Like Ezekiel, we need to move out into deeper waters, so that we swim in a river of life which brings healing to the nations (Ezekiel 47:1ff.). But it takes faith and determination to trust oneself to the deep and it is tempting to stay where we can keep our feet on the sand.

In Ezekiel's vision, there are a thousand cubits between each new depth (47:3ff.). Sometimes, we do not have the perseverance to keep pressing on. We become accustomed to the level where we are and settle there. Remember, the Spirit searches all things, even the depths of God (1 Corinthians 2:9–10). If we want to plumb those depths, we dare not become stranded where we are in the shallows.

This requires ongoing obedience and a yieldedness to everything the Spirit shows us. We cannot walk, pray or live in the Spirit if we are unyielding. The Scripture gives us serious warning:

> *'So, as the Holy Spirit says: "Today, if you hear his voice, do not harden your hearts as you did in the rebellion, during the time of testing in the desert, where your fathers tested and tried me and for forty years saw what I did. That is why I was angry with that generation, and I said, 'Their hearts are always going astray, and they have not known my ways.' So I declared on oath in my anger, 'They shall never enter my rest.'"'*   (Hebrews 3:7–11)

There is a 'rest' in the Spirit-filled life. It brings with it a sense of sweetness, of contentment, of tranquillity, of peace and of fortification against the enemy of our souls. But it also requires obedience. The Holy Spirit Himself says, *'Today, if you hear his voice, do not harden your hearts...'* (Hebrews 3:15). These words are repeated in the fourth chapter of Hebrews. They are critical. Praying in the Spirit involves yieldedness to His word. It means being willing to do whatever He says whenever He says it. It means keeping our hearts soft so we find it easy to say 'yes'.

Do it

So the final principle for praying in the Spirit is, 'Do it!' It is not a suggestion, nor even an invitation. It is a strong, clear command:

> *'Pray in the Spirit on all occasions with all kinds of prayers and requests. With this in mind, be alert and always keep on praying for all the saints.'*   (Ephesians 6:18)

Prayer in the Spirit is a wonderful way of tapping into the resources of the kingdom of God through the Counsellor Jesus promised us. We should take every opportunity to do it.

> **May your spirit be so fused with God's Spirit that when you pray there will be but one voice; may your heart beat so steadily with the rhythm of God that where you live there will be but one life; may your feet tread so naturally in the footsteps of Jesus that where you walk there will be but one track. Amen.**

Don't forget

- Being Spirit-filled is not automatic. It doesn't just happen. The fact that it is a biblical command makes it clear that there is responsibility on our part.

- It is important to realize that both the person and the power of the Holy Spirit are potentially ours.

- The Spirit indwells us to give us life – He comes upon us to empower us for greater effectiveness in service.

- Praying in the Spirit requires ongoing obedience and a yieldedness to everything the Spirit shows us. We cannot walk, pray or live in the Spirit if we are unyielding.

- Praying in the Spirit involves yieldedness to His word. It means being willing to do whatever He says whenever He says it. It means keeping our hearts soft so we find it easy to say 'yes'.

Notes

1   M. Green, *I Believe in the Holy Spirit* (London: Hodder and Stoughton, 1975), p. 119.

2   J.H. Moulton and G. Milligan, *The Vocabulary of the Greek New Testament* (London: Hodder and Stoughton, 1963), pp. 79, 617f.

3   R.J. Knowling, 'The Acts of the Apostles' in W. Nicholl (ed.), *The Expositor's Greek Testament* Volume II (Grand Rapids: Eerdmans, 1967), p. 268.

Chapter 21

'We Constantly Pray for You'
(2 Thessalonians 1:11)

Spiritual exercises

Ignatius Loyola, a one-time soldier who became the founder of the Society of Jesus, commonly known as the Jesuits, laid down for his followers a handbook of military-like instructions that he called *Spiritual Exercises*.

They demanded absolute and unquestioning obedience in everything, not only to God, but also to each other. While most Christians would disagree with Loyola's regimental approach, and would take strong exception to some of what he required, the idea of spiritual exercises is not in itself wrong. In fact, in many ways it has much to commend it. We might well ask the question, 'Wouldn't a programme of spiritual exercises be valuable for all Christians?'

Physical exercise is popular enough these days. And not without reason. The comfortable lifestyle most people lead does not extend us physically. Our bodies need regular toning. Unless we have a job that demands it, most of us drive, ride and sit far more than we should. We need to exercise our bodies regularly.

Many Christians are in the same position spiritually. Our devotional lives are not disciplined. Too often, our only systematic prayer or worship time occurs in church on Sundays. Clinical and pastoral research indicates clearly that the majority of Christians do not have a structured devotional life. We only pray or read the Bible when we feel like it or when we are in need. Of course, there are many exceptions to this, but the problem is widespread enough. Then there are many others who really do try diligently to keep up a daily quiet time, but who find the effort less than successful.

Here is a simple suggested programme of daily spiritual exercises that any reasonably committed Christian should be able to follow. I know from personal experience that it works. (It works for me, anyway.) I hope it will be helpful to you, too.

The nature of prayer

First, you should not try to follow these suggestions legalistically. If, for some reason, you miss out one day, there is no need to feel guilty or condemned. These are guidelines, not regulations! Prayer is basically communion with God. It is a time of friendly interaction with Him. If we regulate it too much, we lose the spontaneity and the intimacy. If, on some occasions, you feel like throwing the exercises out the window and just enjoying a relaxed time with the Lord, that's fine. God is our Father and we are His children, so we need to approach Him appropriately. Nevertheless, we can become undisciplined in our devotional lives. So some structures are helpful in our spiritual formation.

Second, these exercises should not be the only spiritual activity of the day. Obviously, every hour should be lived in fellowship and harmony with the Lord. Normally, you will feel like chatting with God many times before the day is out. But as a concentrated devotional effort, these disciplines can be helpful.

Third, the suggested times are guidelines only. You may choose to spend longer on some parts. But, in my opinion, they should be regarded as minimums. I think you will find anything less inadequate.

Fourth, it is important to choose a suitable place – a spot where you will not be interrupted – such as a study, a verandah, the beach, a park, a church. Be comfortable. Sit, kneel, walk – whatever helps you best to relax with God.

Last, you will need a prayer diary. I suggest a loose-leaf notebook so you can easily add extra pages or replace pages that you need to change. These are readily available from stationers or newsagents. (If you like to walk while you pray, you will need to keep it small.) In time, you will probably have a collection of such books. These will form a valuable record of your spiritual growth and development. (In fact, it could be good to start a new one each year.)

1. Read the Scriptures (*minimum*: 10 minutes)

Follow a systematic programme of Bible reading such as studying a book at a time. One of the many programmes offered by organizations like Scripture Union can be helpful here.

Spend time working with the Word. Ask yourself questions such as the following and note down the answers in your prayer diary:

- What is the main theme of this passage?
- What is its central message?
- What is the key text?
- Is there an example to follow?
- Is there an example to avoid?
- Is there a promise to claim?
- Is there a warning to heed?
- Is there a command to obey?
- What is God saying to me through this passage?

There is no better way I know of to derive the best out of Scripture than asking questions like these. It's a good idea to cast the net of our imagination very wide and to raise every issue we can think of.

Don't be content to ignore or accept uncritically passages you don't understand. Be workmanlike in your approach (2 Timothy 2:15). If I can say this reverently, tease the Scripture. Knead it. Struggle with it. Grapple with it. Be like Jacob, and refuse to let it go until it blesses you (Genesis 32:26)!

2. Memorize a text (*minimum*: 3 minutes)

Choose one text from your reading each week and write it out in your prayer diary. Then memorize it, together with the reference (this is very important). Many people quail at the thought of

Scripture memorization, but it is not nearly as difficult as it seems. The most important thing is repetition. If you spend three minutes a day every day repeating the text, you will learn it easily in a week. Especially if you also write it out on a card or piece of notepaper and glance at it regularly during the day. Another hint – recite the text out aloud. One of the Old Testament words for 'meditate' means to 'mutter'. As we meditate in this way, success is guaranteed (Joshua 1:8; Psalm 119:11, 13, 16).

And don't forget to test yourself. You will never know if you have learned a text unless you try to repeat it from memory without looking at it. If you can remember your birth date or your phone number, you can remember Scripture!

3. Worship the Lord   (*minimum*: 3 minutes)

Sincere worship is the starting point for communion with God (Psalm 100:2; John 4:24). Worship is essentially focused on the Lord Himself. So praise God for who He is. Tell Him you love Him. Thank Him for His presence.

At first, you may find it hard to sustain this for very long (unless you repeat yourself). However, practice makes perfect and as you keep at it, you will soon find that three minutes is nowhere near enough.

Meanwhile, why not use a written expression of adoration – a psalm, a hymn or a written prayer? Sing your worship, if you like.

4. Thank the Lord   (*minimum*: 3 minutes)

Thank God for what He has done for you. No matter what has happened, there is always something to be grateful for. The Bible tells us to give thanks in everything (1 Thessalonians 5:18). Thanksgiving is a form of sacrifice which is acceptable to God (Hebrews 13:15).

Here, again, you may find this hard at first. But if you think of all the blessings in your life and give Him thanks for them, you will soon have no difficulty, especially if you write down a list. Then, as things come to mind – at other times during the day, or while you are in bed at night – jot them down. Your list will soon grow. In particular thank God for the salvation that is ours in Jesus Christ.

5. Confess your sins (*minimum*: 2 minutes)

Apologize to God for sins both of commission and omission. Ask Him to bring things to your notice that you may have over-looked.

Repent of anything which is undermining your first love (Revelation 2:5). Sin cannot destroy our relationship with God – we are still His children – but it can ruin our fellowship. If we confess our sin, that fellowship can be restored (1 John 1:9).

If there is some deliberate sin in your life, you will need to bring it into the light. It is only as we walk in the light that we have fellowship with God and with one another (1 John 1:7). We can never have an effective devotional life if there are areas we have not faced up to.

This especially applies to unresolved bitterness or resentment which can be crippling and destructive. The writer to the Hebrews warns us that we should not allow any root of bitter-ness to spring up within us (Hebrews 12:15) and Jesus tells us plainly that unforgiveness towards others will short-circuit God's forgiveness towards us (Matthew 5:23f.; Mark 11:25; see also Ephesians 4:32; 1 Peter 3:7).

6. Accept His forgiveness (*minimum*: 2 minutes)

Praise God that He has already forgiven you in Christ. Meditate on the many passages of Scripture that promise you forgiveness through the blood of Jesus (e.g. Romans 5:8; Ephesians 1:7; Colossians 1:20; Hebrews 7:25; Revelation 7:14).

Rejoice that you are a child of God, a member of His family, secure in His love and kept by His grace. It's a good idea to read passages like Ephesians chapter one over and over, in order to know beyond a doubt that in Christ we have every spiritual blessing we can ever need. Make a list of these promises and blessings in your prayer diary.

Repeat these promises with enthusiasm. Don't be afraid to get a bit excited!

7. Pray with the spirit (*minimum*: 5 minutes)

When we pray in our own language, we are praying with the mind. When we pray in a tongue, it is the spirit praying (1 Corinthians 14:14). For a full-orbed prayer life it is important to spend time speaking in tongues. Cultivate your prayer language. Use it to develop your intimacy with God. Persist until you know you are praying effectively. As your spirit communes with the Lord, your heart will begin to rise up with faith and joy as you sense His presence. This may not happen immediately. You may need much more than five minutes before your awareness of spiritual intimacy develops. So don't stop too soon!

Also, don't assume that you should always speak in the same tongue. In his list of charismata, Paul includes *'different kinds of tongues'* (1 Corinthians 12:10). You should expect to speak different languages at different times, depending on the Spirit's direction. And listen to your heart as you pray. Let your feelings come through. Speak with emotion, with feeling, with compassion, with worship – don't just blurt it out! By faith, use new words and forms or expression.

8. Pray for the needs of others (*minimum*: 5 minutes)

In your prayer dairy, draw up a list of people you can pray for each day. At first, you may not have a long list, but once you start, it will grow. Every day, you will think of other names you can add. You can have different categories of people each day – family, friends, missionaries, politicians, church leaders, workmates and so on. Also, you can draw on other prayer lists (e.g. from mission organizations) as a resource.

To pray for one another is part of being a Christian – we are clearly instructed to pray for all the saints (Ephesians 6:18) and failure to do so is a sin (1 Samuel 12:23).

9. Pray for your own need (*minimum*: 3 minutes)

Jesus told us to pray for God to meet our daily needs (Luke 11:3). So it is quite in order to bring them before God. Of all the things we pray for, our own needs are probably the easiest to remember! They usually remind us very plainly of their presence. Name them clearly and ask God to meet them. If you are not sure what to ask for, pray in tongues until you feel the Lord has heard you. It's also a good idea to list your needs in your prayer diary and cross them off when they are met.

10. Pray for guidance   (*minimum*: 5 minutes)

It is vital to live each day according to the will of God. Most of the time, we can assume that we are being led by the Spirit – we have His promise that this is the case (Romans 8:14; Isaiah 58:11). But it is still important to commit the day to the Lord and to ask Him for guidance. Try to ascertain His will for you.

Seek His direction. Listen for His voice – He may have new directions He wants to give you. Then claim the day for God!

This is especially important if you are faced with a difficult decision. Talk it over with God as you would with a friend. Lay out the various options and ask Him to help you sort them out. You may not receive an answer straight away, but you can expect the assurance that it's all under control and that the answer will come (Isaiah 30:21).

The value of spiritual exercises

By observing these simple exercises, you will spend over thirty minutes a day focusing on your spiritual formation. Of course, often, you will spend longer. The times suggested are minimums only. You may spend thirty minutes just praying with the spirit or reading the Scripture. And at other times during the day, you will obviously pray, read God's Word, and so on.

By the end of twelve months, you will have achieved the following:

- you will know how to worship the Lord better
- you will have a comprehensive prayer list
- you will know over 50 verses of Scripture by heart
- you will be disciplined in your prayer life
- you will be spiritually healthy
- you will have a more intimate relationship with the Lord.

These accomplishments speak for themselves. So, then, let's pray!

Don't forget

A daily schedule

- Read the Scriptures (10 min.).
- Memorize a text (3 min.).
- Worship the Lord (3 min.).
- Thank the Lord (3 min.).
- Confess your sins (2 min.).
- Accept His forgiveness (2 min.).
- Pray with the spirit (5 min.).
- Pray for the needs of others (5 min.).
- Pray for your own need (3 min.).
- Pray for guidance (5 min.).

'Do you not know that in a race all the runners run, but only one gets the prize? Run in such a way as to get the prize. Everyone who competes in the games goes into strict training. They do it to get a crown that will not last; but we do it to get a crown that will last for ever. Therefore I do not run like a man running aimlessly; I do not fight like a man beating the air. No, I beat my body and make it my slave so that after I have preached to others, I myself will not be disqualified for the prize.'

(1 Corinthians 9:24–27)

Appendix A

'According to the Spirit'
(Romans 8:4)

The meaning of the word 'spirit' in the New Testament

Is glossolalia praying 'in the Spirit' or 'with the spirit' or both?

Human or holy?

Part of our difficulty lies in the fact that, as we have noted, it is not always obvious whether the New Testament is talking about the human spirit or the Holy Spirit, especially when the subject is prayer. Of course, in some settings the distinction is clear. When the epithet 'holy' is used with the word 'spirit' then it is clearly the Holy Spirit who is intended (e.g. Acts 1:8; 2:4; Romans 5:5; 1 Corinthians 6:19; Ephesians 4:30, etc.). Similarly, when phrases like 'Spirit of God' are used, there is no doubt of the intention. So it is only by God's Spirit that can we call Jesus 'Lord' (1 Corinthians 12:3). In other cases, the context makes it plain that the Holy Spirit is the subject. It is the Spirit who leads us (Galatians 5:18); love is bedded in the Spirit (Colossians 1:8); by the Spirit we are sanctified (2 Thessalonians 2:13); and the Spirit warns us (1 Timothy 4:1).

On other occasions, the reference is clearly to the human spirit. So several times, Paul writes, *'The grace of the Lord Jesus Christ be with your spirit'* or, *'The Lord be with your spirit'* (Galatians 6:18; Philippians 4:23; 2 Timothy 4:22; Philemon 25). He talks of the spirit being saved (1 Corinthians 5:4, 5; 1 Thessalonians 5:23) or quite specifically of the spirit of a man

(1 Corinthians 2:11). To the Romans, he uses the adjective 'my' with the word 'spirit' (Romans 1:9 RSV) as he does to the Corinthians (1 Corinthians 14:14). In all these cases, it is obvious that the word 'spirit' should be rendered with a lower case 's'.

There is a third group of texts, however, where it is unclear whether the Holy Spirit or the human spirit is intended. One of these is the well-known passage in Galatians which talks of the fruit of the Spirit. Here, again, there is nothing in the words themselves to indicate whether the apostle is talking of fruit of the Holy Spirit or fruit developing from a renewed human spirit (Galatians 5:16ff.). The whole section can be read either way. In the ultimate, of course, all spiritual fruit finds its origin in the Holy Spirit who makes us alive and therefore able to be fruitful. But even so, Paul could be thinking of a renewed human spirit which has for the first time begun to bear a crop.

Similarly, in the eighth chapter of Romans, there is ambiguity in the Greek text. Without exception, Bible translations take the word *pneuma* to refer to the Holy Spirit. However, this is not as obvious as it first seems. In verse 9, for example, the word refers to the Spirit of God and in verse 10 to the spirit of man!

At the beginning of the chapter, there is a strong contrast drawn between the spirit and the flesh. This is normally taken to mean God's Spirit and human flesh. But as the flesh is human, might not the spirit also be human? Certainly, the Greek text is fully capable of this understanding. Then as the passage proceeds, the emphasis changes to the Holy Spirit. For interest, try reading these few verses in this way:

> *'And so he condemned sin in sinful man, in order that the righteous requirements of the law might be fully met in us, who do not live according to the flesh but according to the* [renewed] *spirit. Those who live according to the flesh have their minds set on what the flesh desires; but those who live in accordance with the* [renewed] *spirit have their minds set on what the* [renewed] *spirit desires. The mind of the flesh is death, but the mind controlled by the* [renewed] *spirit is life and peace; the sinful mind is hostile to God . . .*
>
> *You, however, are controlled not by the flesh but by the* [renewed] *spirit, if the Spirit of God lives in you. And if anyone*

does not have the Spirit of Christ, he does not belong to Christ. But if Christ is in you, your body is dead because of sin, yet your [renewed] *spirit is alive because of righteousness. And if the Spirit of him who raised Jesus from the dead is living in you, he who raised Christ from the dead will also give life to your mortal bodies through his Spirit, who lives in you.'* (Romans 8:1–11)

I am not trying to argue that the word *pneuma* should be understood in this way: just that it is possible.[1]

With the spirit

Back to prayer. As we have seen, to the Corinthians, Paul mentions several times that speaking in tongues is praying with the spirit. As in Romans 8, *pneuma* occurs in reference to both the human spirit and the Holy Spirit: In 1 Corinthians 14 he writes:

*'For anyone who speaks in a tongue does not speak to men but to God. Indeed, no one understands him; he utters mysteries **with his spirit**.'* (1 Corinthians 14:2)

*'For if I pray in a tongue, **my spirit prays**, but my mind is unfruitful. So what shall I do?'* (1 Corinthians 14:14–15a)

*'I will pray **with my spirit**, but I will also pray with my mind; I will sing **with my spirit**, but I will also sing with my mind.'* (1 Corinthians 14:15b)

*'If you are praising God **with your spirit**, how can one who finds himself among those who do not understand say "Amen" to your thanksgiving, since he does not know what you are saying?'* (1 Corinthians 14:16)

Only in verses 14 and 15 is it beyond question that Paul is referring to the human spirit. In the Greek text, verse 14 is the only passage where the personal pronoun 'my' is used. In verse 15, the contrast with the mind again indicates clearly that it is the human spirit to which he refers.

In the other verses, it would be equally valid to use the word 'Spirit'. Hence, the New International Version translation of verse 2 (above) uses *'his spirit'*, as does the New King James Version, while the Revised Standard Version uses *'the Spirit'*. The context, however, seems to me to argue favourably for the human spirit in each case. Like the New International Version, the Revised Standard Version follows this approach in verses 15 and 16.

A similar point can be made regarding Paul's teaching about inexpressible prayer in Romans 8:26–27. Here, too, we could render the word *pneuma* as 'spirit' rather than 'Spirit'. In fact, given that Paul uses the pronoun 'itself' rather than (as in most English translations) 'himself', and that it is by searching our hearts that God discovers the prayer, this could be a preferred translation:

> *'In the same way, the* [human] *spirit helps us in our weakness. We do not know what we ought to pray for, but the spirit itself intercedes for us with groans that words cannot express. And he who searches our hearts knows the mind of the spirit, because the spirit intercedes for the saints in accordance with God's will.'*

Generally scholars prefer to see this passage as referring to the Holy Spirit, and the context suggests that it does. But we are still left with a degree of ambiguity.

There may be a clue in the fact that the Greek phrase *en pneumati* ('in Spirit') is nearly always used about being immersed in the Holy Spirit (Matthew 3:11; Luke 3:16; Acts 1:5; 1 Corinthians 12:13). It is also the word-form employed in Ephesians 3:5 and Colossians 1:8, both of which refer to the Holy Spirit. On the other hand, in the verses from Corinthians quoted above, Paul uses the instrumental dative, and so it is 'with the spirit' that Paul prays in tongues.

Even this is not clear-cut, however, as Paul uses the phrase *en pneumati* in 1 Corinthians 14:16, which is plainly a continuation of his discussion about praying 'with' his own spirit. Furthermore, he writes *en to pneumati* in Romans 1:9, where the reference is clearly to his own human spirit, which is obvious by the use of the pronoun 'my'. And to go back to Romans 8 and Galatians 5, the instrumental dative is also used there even though the reference may be to the Holy Spirit!

Similar comments may be made about Ephesians 6:18:

> *'And pray in the Spirit on all occasions with all kinds of prayers and requests. With this in mind, be alert and always keep on praying for all the saints.'*

In the Greek text, the phrase is literally and simply 'in spirit' (*en pneumati*). This is the grammatical form normally used in reference to being baptized in the Holy Spirit. So in this case, both the New International Version and New Revised Standard Version opt for 'Spirit'. And as we have seen, this passage talks about all kinds of prayers, not just glossolalia.

Similarly, when Jude talks about praying in the Spirit, not only is the phraseology identical, but the addition of the word 'holy' clearly specifies the Holy Spirit (Jude 20 – *en pneumati hagio*). So also, Paul's reference to worship in the Spirit is specifically 'in the Spirit of God' (Philippians 3:3).

Nevertheless, because of the inconsistency in usage we have already noted, it could be argued we should translate Ephesians 6:18, 'Pray with the spirit . . . ' – in other words, pray in tongues. And there is no doubt that this is, at the very least, one of the forms of prayer to which Paul refers.

Dilemma

So we are still left with some degree of uncertainty about the correct translation. The dilemma is heightened by the fact that only a handful of biblical commentators discuss the issue. In regard to Romans chapter 8, Robertson prefers the Holy Spirit but concedes it could be 'the renewed spirit of man'.[2] Lenski presents a slightly different perspective when he blends both views by taking *pneuma* to refer to the whole realm of the spirit including both human and holy spirit.[3]

Commenting on 1 Corinthians 14, Gordon Fee sees such an intimate connection between the action of the human spirit and the activation of the Holy Spirit that he coins the term 'S/spirit'. He puts it like this:

> ' . . . the difficult wording "my spirit prays" seems to mean something like "my S/spirit prays." On the one hand, both

the possessive "my" and the contrast with "my mind" indicate he [Paul] is here referring to his own "spirit" at prayer. On the other hand, there can be little question, on the basis of the combined evidence of 12:7–11 and 14:2 and 16, that Paul understood speaking in tongues to be an activity of the Spirit in one's life; it is prayer and praise directed toward God in the language of Spirit-inspiration. The most viable solution to this ambiguity is that by the language "my spirit prays" Paul means his own spirit is praying as the Holy Spirit gives the utterance. Hence, "my S/spirit prays."' [4]

Ken Chant leans strongly towards an emphasis on the human spirit. Indeed, he argues that from these references we may infer that

'. . . just as the human mind possesses an inherent ability to express itself through a known language, so the human spirit possesses an inherent ability to express itself through an unknown language.' [5]

Rienecker simply notes that Paul may be referring to either the human spirit or the Holy Spirit or 'the spiritual gift given by the Holy Spirit'. [6]

Co-operation

So speaking in tongues is a manifestation of the Spirit (1 Corinthians 12:7). The word 'manifestation' means 'revealing' or 'making known'. To put it differently, the Spirit makes known something which has previously been buried.

Moreover, it is also important to stress that what the Spirit gives is *'kinds of tongues'* (1 Corinthians 12:10), not 'the gift of tongues', a phrase which nowhere occurs in the New Testament.

Just as words of wisdom or discernings of spirits are both natural and spiritual abilities, so are various kinds of tongues. True, they are charismata, but they are also linked closely with fundamental Christian qualities.

This partly explains why glossolalia may occur in pagan rites and hypnotic trances. There is an innate ability there, and somehow it is touched off by the ritual. In this case, however, the prayer content is absent and very likely, given the ruinous condition of the human spirit, there is either a demonic component or a fleshly attempt to express the cry of the spirit.

Furthermore, the extensive instructions given in the letter to the Corinthians make it obvious that glossolalia is subject to human control – like any other human ability. Clearly, if praying in a tongue were entirely up to the Holy Spirit, it would be impossible for us to do anything to start, stop or modulate it. But as it is a human ability, activated by the Holy Spirit, we can do all of those things freely at any time.

Speaking in a tongue is an expression of a remarkable co-operation between the human spirit and the Holy Spirit. To use a colloquialism, it is the best of both worlds. Once we realize this, texts which are not normally associated with glossolalia now spring to mind such as:

> 'The [Holy] *Spirit himself testifies with our spirit that we are God's children.'* (Romans 8:16)

> '. . . *he who unites himself with the Lord is one with him in spirit.'* (1 Corinthians 6:17)

I am not suggesting these statements are direct references to praying in tongues. But when we see glossolalia in this way, such statements do take on new meaning.

Because glossolalia is an activity of the human spirit, it is subject to the human will. It originates neither in the will nor the mind, but it is under the control of both. Just as we may decide to pray with words that stem from our minds, so we may also decide to pray with words that derive from our spirits. And this is important. While prayers that originate in our minds may be diluted or even worse, polluted, by our own desires, praying that rises from the spirit can only occur with the help of the Holy Spirit. This is why we may use the term 'prayer language' to describe this phenomenon.

It is clear that all genuine prayer is 'in the Holy Spirit'. There is no other way to pray. But it is also clear that prayer 'with the spirit' is specifically praying in tongues as the Spirit gives the ability.

Notes

1   Compare A. Robertson, *Word Pictures in the New Testament* (Nashville: Broadman Press, 1931), pp. 373f.

2   ibid., p. 373.

3   R.C.H. Lenski, *The Interpretation of St Paul's Epistle to the Romans* (Minneapolis: Augsburg, 1961), p. 502.

4   G. Fee, *The First Epistle to the Corinthians* (Grand Rapids: Eerdmans, 1987), p. 670.

5   K. Chant, *Clothed with Power* (Kingswood, NSW: Ken Chant Ministries, 1993), p. 116.

6   F. Rienecker, *A Linguistic Key to the Greek New Testament* (Regency, 1980), p. 435.

Bibliography

Anderson, Robert, *Vision of the Disinherited* (New York: Oxford, 1979).

Arnold, Matthew, *Literature and Dogma* (1873).

Augustine of Hippo, *Confession*, I, 1.

Barnes, A., *Notes on the New Testament* (Chicago: Moody, 1968).

Behm, J., 'Parakaleo' in G. Friedrich (ed.), *Theological Dictionary of the New Testament* (Grand Rapids: Eerdmans, 1968).

Billheimer, P., *Destined for the Throne* (London: CLC, 1975).

Bingham, G., *Come Let Us Pray* (Blackwood: New Creation, 1988).

Bittlinger, A., *Gifts and Graces* (London: Hodder and Stoughton, 1967).

Budgen, V., *The Charismatics and the Word of God* (Welwyn: Evangelical Press, 1986).

Calvin, John, *Institutes*, III, 5.

Chant, B., *Your Guide to God's Power* (Tonbridge: Sovereign World, 1986).

Chant, K., *Clothed with Power* (Kingswood, NSW: Ken Chant Ministries, 1993).

Cho, P.Y., *Praying With Jesus* (Word, 1987).

Christenson, L., *Welcome, Holy Spirit* (Augsburg, 1987).

Chrysostom, John, *Homilies on Romans*, 14; *Homilies on 1 Corinthians* 35.

Denney, J., 'St Paul's Epistle to the Romans' in *The Expositor's Greek Testament*, Volume II (Grand Rapids: Eerdmans, 1967).

Edwards, J., *The Religious Affections* (Edinburgh: The Banner of Truth Trust, [1746] 1984).

Fee, G., *The First Epistle to the Corinthians* (Grand Rapids: Eerdmans, 1987).

God's Empowering Presence: the Holy Spirit in the Letters of Paul (Peabody, Mass.: Henrickson, 1994).

Listening to the Spirit in the Text (Grand Rapids: Eerdmans, 2000).

Findlay, G.G., 'St Paul's First Epistle to the Corinthians' in *The Expositor's Greek Testament* Volume II (Grand Rapids: Eerdmans, 1967).

Fitzpatrick, G., *How to Recognize God's Voice* (Tonbridge: Sovereign World, 2001).

Freud, S., 'The Unconscious' in *Great Books of the Western World Volume 54, Freud* (Encyclopaedia Britannica, 1952).

Friedrich, G. (ed), *Theological Dictionary of the New Testament* (Grand Rapids: Eerdmans, 1972).

Green, M., *I Believe in the Holy Spirit* (London: Hodder and Stoughton, 1975).

Hallesby, O., *Prayer* (IVF, 1948).

Henry, Matthew, *Matthew Henry's Commentary* (New York: Fleming H. Revell, n.d.).

Hummel, C., *Fire in the Fireplace* (Downers Grove: IVP, 1978).

Irenaeus, *Against Heresies*, 5, 6, 1.

Julian of Norwich, *Revelations of Divine Love* (London: Hodder and Stoughton, 1987).

Kelsey, M., *Tongue-Speaking: the History and Meaning of Charismatic Experience* (New York: Crossroad, 1981).

Kenneally, C., *Other Tongues*, unpublished thesis (University of Melbourne, 1990).

Lenski, R.C.H., *The Interpretation of St Paul's Epistle to the Romans* (Minneapolis: Augsburg, 1961).

Liddell and Scott, *A Lexicon (abridged)* (London: Oxford, 1872).

Macchia, F., 'Sighs Too Deep for Words,' *Journal of Pentecostal Theology* 1 (October 1992).

Mills, W. (ed.), *Speaking in Tongues: A Guide to Research in Glossolalia* (Grand Rapids: Eerdmans, 1986).

Moorhead, M.W., *A Cloud of Witnesses to Pentecost in India*, Pamphlet no. 4, (Bombay, 1908).

Moulton, J.H., and Milligan, G., *The Vocabulary of the Greek New Testament* (London: Hodder and Stoughton, 1963).

Murray, J., *The Epistle to the Romans* (Grand Rapids: Eerdmans, 1973).

Nicholl, W.R., *The Expositor's Greek Testament*, Volumes II and III (Grand Rapids: Eerdmans, 1967).

Perschbacher, W.J. (ed.), *The New Analytical Greek Lexicon* (Peabody, Mass.: Hendrickson, 1990).

Pollock, J., *Moody Without Sankey* (London: Hodder and Stoughton, 1963).

Pullinger, J., *Chasing the Dragon* (London: Hodder and Stoughton, 1983).

The Crack in the Wall: the life and death of Kowloon Walled City (London: Hodder and Stoughton, 1989).

Ridderbos, H., *The Epistle of Paul to the Churches of Galatia* in *The New International Commentary on the New Testament* (Grand Rapids: Eerdmans, 1972).

Rienecker, F., *A Linguistic Key to the Greek New Testament* (Regency,1980).

Rinker, R., *Prayer: Conversing with God* (Grand Rapids: Zondervan, 1959).

Roberts, A. and Donaldson, J. (eds.), *The Anti-Nicene Fathers*, Volume I (Grand Rapids: Eerdmans, 1979).

Robertson. A.T., *Word Pictures in the New Testament* (Nashville: Broadman Press, 1931).

Samarin, W., *Tongues of Men and Angels* (Macmillan, 1972).

Schaff, P. (ed.), *The Nicene and Post-Nicene Fathers* Volumes XI and XII (Grand Rapids: Eerdmans, 1979).

Sheldrake, E. (ed.), *The Personal Letters of John Alexander Dowie* (Zion City: W.G. Voliva, 1912).

Stagg, F., Hinson, E.G., and Oates, W. (eds.), *Glossolalia: Tongue Speaking in Biblical, Historical and Psychological Perspective* (Abingdon, 1967).

Virkler, M., *Dialogue with God* (Peacemakers, 1987).

Wallis, A., *Pray in the Spirit* (Victory Press, 1975).

Wordsworth, W., *Lyrical Ballads*, 1798.

If you have enjoyed
this book and would like
to help us send a copy of
it and many other titles to
needy pastors in developing nations,

please write for further information,
or send your gift to:

Sovereign World Trust
PO Box 777
Tonbridge
Kent TN11 0ZS
United Kingdom

www.sovereignworldtrust.com